Better Paragraphs Plus

Better Paragraphs Plus

Sixth Edition

John Ostrom
Formerly of Wittenberg University

William Cook

Harper & Row, Publishers, New York
Cambridge, Philadelphia, San Francisco, Washington,
London, Mexico City, São Paulo, Singapore, Sydney

Sponsoring Editor: Barbara Cinquegrani
Project Editor: Jo-Ann Goldfarb
Text Design: Laura Ferguson
Cover Design: Cavalieri Graphics
Production Manager: Jeanie Berke
Production Assistant: Beth Ackerman
Compositor: ComCom Division of Haddon Craftsmen, Inc.
Printer and Binder: R. R. Donnelley & Sons Company
Cover Printer: Lynn Art Offset Corporation

Better Paragraphs Plus, Sixth Edition

This book was previously published in 1983 as *Better Paragraphs and Short Themes,* Fifth Edition.

Library of Congress Cataloging-in-Publication Data

Ostrom, John Ward
  Better paragraphs plus.

  Rev. ed. of: Better paragraphs and short themes.
5th ed. c1983.
  Includes index
  1. English language—Paragraphs. 2. English language—
Rhetoric. I. Cook, William (William W.) II. Ostrom,
John Ward. Better paragraphs and short
themes. III. Title.
PE1439.08 1988   808'.042   87–17813
ISBN 0-06-044973-X

  88 89 90 9 8 7 6 5 4 3 2

▌Contents

▌Preface

The Sixth Edition of *Better Paragraphs and Short Themes,* now titled *Better Paragraphs Plus,* continues a tradition of teaching and learning a valuable writing skill that began some fifty years ago. It carefully preserves the basic techniques of paragraph writing long tested in previous editions. While the ways in which we use language have changed over the years, certain techniques remain invaluable. It may be an oversimplification to say so, but the ability to write an effective paragraph continues to depend on two commands: first, clearly tell the reader what you want to say; then, support your statement with pertinent details, illustrations, and/or reasons.

This edition proceeds on the premise that good writing is a manifestation of effective thinking. Just as the wandering mind produces no organized thought, writing that wanders only confuses the reader. At the heart of this book is a discipline—we call it the *controlling idea.* It is a means of ensuring that the paragraphs you write will say what you want them to say in a way that your reader has a right to expect. The controlling idea will help you not only in writing the answer to essay questions, term papers, and other school requirements, but in similar challenges throughout your career.

What *Better Paragraphs Plus* has to teach is fundamental to the writer who is called upon to explain something to others without confusing them or wasting their time. The paragraph is an effective unit of composition for the teaching of writing because its organization and analyses are controlled and attainable. It is, as well, the basic unit upon which most writing is based.

Material on writing a short composition, adopted in the Fifth Edition, is continued here. The organizational principles used in writing are essentially those of the paragraph. Thus, writing a short composition employs skills learned in paragraph writing and gives the student an opportunity to put those skills to an even wider practical use.

Previous editions were written primarily for the traditional student in the typical classroom setting. The present edition is also designed to serve those persons who may need a self-teaching text. It will, however, be useful also to those who in their daily activities must write reports, memoranda, and correspondence—in fact, to anyone who must explain, clarify, report, or advise in writing.

Ultimately, the ability to write well depends on practice in writing. Having composed something, the effective writer will analyze the result and revise. Many of the examples in this book present, first, a paragraph that does not meet the test of the controlling idea, an analysis of this paragraph, and a rewritten version of it. The topics contained in the various exercises are suggestive only; the authors well recognize that most people write best about topics that interest them.

For instance, one technique, which the classroom teacher might like to consider, is that of creating or simulating "real life" situations. In response, the student is challenged to compose from scratch a carefully written paragraph. Such practice tends to give all student writers a special sense of achievement. The nontraditional student may well have already been faced with the problem of having to explain something clearly in the "real world."

The authors would like to thank the following individuals whose comments were helpful in shaping the sixth edition: Marvin Diogenes, The University of Arizona; Kathy M. Murray, The University of Mississippi; and Robert E. Yarber, San Diego Mesa College.

Finally, to all of you who use this book and want to "say what you mean and mean what you say," good luck! *Better Paragraphs Plus* will be a decided plus for you.

John Ostrom
William Cook

Better Paragraphs Plus

1.
Paragraph
Unity

First, what *is* a paragraph? A narrow definition is not very useful, but there are characteristics of a paragraph that make it distinct from other units of writing. Essentially, a paragraph consists of several sentences supporting a *controlling idea* that is expressed in the *topic sentence* of the paragraph. To achieve paragraph unity, the writer will test each sentence to ensure that it supports the controlling idea.

At this point, narrow definition *is* important. A *controlling idea* is a word, phrase, or clause that identifies precisely what the paragraph is about; for example, a lawnmower, a football team, or something as abstract as national pride. It is the point of the paragraph—what it is all about. "Controlling" is just what it sounds like. If the controlling idea of a paragraph is specifically about football, there is no place in that paragraph for comments about baseball.

The *topic sentence* is essential to a paragraph. It states the controlling idea and provides the field of reference in which the controlling idea will work. It is the writer's way of saying what will be "playing" in the paragraph itself, much in the way that a theater marquee tells you what movie will be showing inside.

The paragraph discusses a single, limited topic that is usually a part of a larger topic. A paragraph is commonly identified by an indented first line, as in the paragraph you are now reading. There is no specified length for a paragraph. It must be long enough to support or clarify the controlling idea, but it must avoid statements not relevant to that idea.

Paragraphing is a way of clarifying for the reader the stages in the writer's thinking. In fairness to the reader, each paragraph must focus attention on a single topic, or on one related part of a larger topic. Sentences in a paragraph that have no clear relationship to one another are merely confusing.

Possibly the greatest mistake a writer can make is the attempt to handle an overly broad topic in a single paragraph. Obviously, a size-twelve foot will not go into a size-nine shoe. But, just as any one part is smaller than the whole, the smaller topic will have its limitations dictated by the nature of the larger topic.

Two essential characteristics of the paragraph already mentioned are the *topic sentence* and the *controlling idea*. Paragraphs, unlike longer writings, do not have titles centered above them. They do, however, have directional signals that we call *controlling ideas*. At this point, a simple example might help. The purpose of it is to illustrate the very important idea of limiting what can be said in a paragraph in the context of a broader topic—in this case, a short paper.

You have been assigned a short paper on the topic, "Why the United States should continue the space program." You might very well use this topic as your thesis statement, a term we will discuss later when we more fully consider the short paper. Right now you must come up with, say, three reasons for why we should support a space program. They might be

1. A successful space program contributes to the *American sense of pride* in national achievement.
2. The program has, after all, been *successful in the past* and, for that reason alone, it should be continued in the future.
3. The space program has made invaluable contributions to *technological development* unrelated to the program itself.

All of these "reasons" are sufficiently limited in scope to allow us to write a paragraph on each of them. Also, each might serve as the topic sentence. Notice that the controlling idea is italicized.

The first reason has a very subjective controlling idea. Still, it is a valid one. Americans *were* a proud people that morning when astronaut Neil Armstrong stepped off the ladder and became the first human being to set foot on the moon. And no doubt the people of the world looked with admiration on the nation that had achieved this remarkable feat.

The second reason might be supported by enumerating several notable achievements of the space program. It is not enough to *say* that the program has been successful; you must *prove* it with examples. Only then will your assertion that the program must be continued because of its past successes be validated. The third reason should be developed in the same way, by describing specific technological advances that have come out of the space program.

Now let us use the controlling idea as a testing method. Which of the following statements support, or do not support, one of the three controlling ideas that we have developed?

1. In the Soviet Union, those we call "astronauts" are called "cosmonauts."
2. Today it is possible for the ambulatory victims of heart attacks to roam about the hospital while their heart performance is monitored in a central place.
3. President Kennedy's stated dream of putting a man on the moon *did* come true.
4. Someday space travel may be a commonplace experience for many Americans.
5. Space is becoming cluttered with the hardware the program has put there.

The first sentence may be true, but it has nothing to do with either national pride, success, or technological development. The second sentence, on the other hand, clearly demonstrates the technological advances in telemetry that have been of benefit to many Americans and others. The fulfillment of President Kennedy's dream is today cited as an example of what a nation can do through singleness of purpose. It clearly supports the controlling idea of American pride. Sentences 4 and 5, on the other hand, do not support any of our controlling ideas.

At this point you might wonder which should be developed first, the controlling idea or the topic sentence. Remember that we compared the controlling idea with the title of a longer composition. For this reason, the controlling idea should come first. Then the topic sentence is developed as a vehicle for it. To go back to our example, the three controlling ideas, *American pride, successful in the past,* and *technological advancements* might have been mere jottings on your writing pad.

Two more fairly detailed examples of paragraph development follow. By studying them carefully, you will begin to see a pattern emerging in the limitation of the topic and the use of the controlling idea as a testing method.

Let us suppose that after a trip or a session with an atlas you have decided to write a paragraph about the names of American cities and towns. It strikes you that many of them are familiar, not from the names of the cities or towns themselves, but from some other source. Remember that you are now in the thinking and planning stage. You jot down an idea for a topic sentence that might read as follows:

Anyone who travels much (or studies an atlas) in the United States soon realizes that towns and cities often have familiar names.

Such a sentence, placed first in a paragraph, presumably would serve as a generalized topic sentence. It contains your controlling idea, *familiar names,* and states in a broad way what the paragraph will be about. The problem is, both the controlling idea and, in consequence, the topic sentence are a little too broad. Our next job, therefore, is to limit them to what can be handled in a paragraph. It is a task very much like using a special lens on a camera to "zoom" in on some *particular part* of the picture you would otherwise be taking. By doing so, you get a clearer picture of that particular part. You get a depth of concentration.

Your topic sentence, therefore, should include some central point that you wish to stress concerning those names. After considering several possibilities, you may decide that the towns and cities you are really interested in have namesakes in various parts of the world. You now adjust your topic sentence to something like this:

Anyone who travels throughout the United States soon realizes that towns and cities have namesakes here at home and abroad.

Although this is a more limited topic sentence, still further limitation is needed. The United States is, after all, a very large country, with thousands of towns and cities. To keep the paragraph manageable, you might consider geographical limitation. For example, you might decide to limit your paragraph to namesakes in states east of the Mississippi River. Another obvious limitation, which would also serve as a kindness to your reader, would be to discuss only *famous* namesakes. Here is an even more restricted topic sentence:

People traveling in states east of the Mississippi River soon realize that certain towns and cities on their itinerary have famous namesakes here and abroad.

"Famous namesakes" is now your main point or *controlling idea.* Notice that it is much more limited in scope than was the idea of "familiar names."

Your chief concern in writing this particular paragraph, therefore, is to choose a city like London, Ohio: first, because it has London, England, as a famous namesake and, second, because Ohio is east of the Mississippi River. Any London *west* of the Mississippi must not be included, even though it would meet your controlling-idea test, because it is not within the geographical limits established by your topic sentence.

A topic sentence with a definite *controlling idea* is the first requirement of ultimate paragraph unity. And notice that the emphasis is on "controlling idea." Unless *all* of the material you include in the paragraph supports or proves the controlling idea in terms of the rest of the topic sentence, the paragraph will not be unified. The following paragraph is not unified, for the writer included material which not only fails to follow the controlling idea but detracts from it. That material should be fairly obvious to you.

> People traveling in states east of the Mississippi River soon realize that certain towns and cities on their itinerary have famous namesakes here at home and abroad. Since the more populous states are in the East, there are more names from which to choose. Georgia and Florida have a Milton, Illinois a Carlyle, New York a Homer and an Ovid, and Pennsylvania a Seneca. Many students know that Milton was blind when he wrote *Paradise Lost.* A Columbus is found in Arkansas and Georgia, a De Soto and La Salle in Illinois, and a Ponce de León in Florida. Even today the Fountain of Youth, which Ponce de León discovered, produces a million gallons of water each hour. Washington appears in eleven states, among which are Connecticut, Indiana, Kentucky, Michigan, North Carolina, Virginia, and, of course, the District of Columbia. Eight states claim a Lincoln, including Alabama, Maine, Mississippi, New Hampshire, and Vermont. One might expect to find a Lincoln in Kentucky, since he was born near Hodgenville in a cabin still preserved in a granite memorial there. From prominent ancient cities Illinois selected Athens, Rome, Sparta, and Troy; New York chose Athens, Babylon, Ithaca, Rome, and Troy. In fact, Troy appears in no less than eight other eastern states: Alabama, Michigan, Indiana, New Hampshire, North Carolina, Ohio, Pennsylvania, and Tennessee. Texans may have been motivated by a sequential optimism when they named six of their communities Earth, Eden, Tranquility, Happy, Blessing, and Paradise, to say nothing of Rail Road Flat and Scenic Loop Playground.

There are several items in this paragraph that do little or nothing to develop the controlling idea, "famous namesakes," or are inconsistent with the topic sentence, which specifies states *east* of the Mississippi River. Therefore,

1. There should be no references to Arkansas or Texas.
2. There should be no reference to Milton's blindness, the Fountain of Youth, or the Lincoln Memorial in Hodgenville, because they do nothing to support the controlling idea.
3. There should be no place names such as those mentioned in Texas, because they do not have famous namesakes (with the possible exception of Earth and Eden, which would more properly go in a paragraph on, say, *colorful* place names).

The paragraph still tries to cover too much ground even with the irrelevant material taken out. The result is a paragraph that lacks organization. Again, the writer must further limit the material to be covered. This could be done by eliminating the words "here at home," which would allow the writer to concentrate only on namesakes from abroad. To do so, of course, would eliminate places named for Washington and Lincoln, but other foreign names, such as Bismarck, Elizabeth, and Napoleon, could be easily substituted.

The topic sentence of a paragraph makes a commitment to the reader. That commitment is to deliver in an organized fashion whatever details, reasons, illustrations, or other evidence you think appropriate.

While it may not be apparent in the paragraph we just examined, there is a degree of organization to it. Note the following:

WRITERS	EXPLORERS	CENTERS OF ANCIENT CULTURE
Milton	Columbus	Athens
Carlyle	De Soto	Rome
Homer	La Salle	Sparta
Ovid	Ponce de León	Troy
Seneca		Babylon
		Ithaca

We have, of course, omitted the *American* statesmen, Washington and Lincoln, and for them substituted:

FOREIGN STATESMEN
> Bismarck
>
> Elizabeth
>
> Napoleon

Now, with this classification scheme in mind, we will revise the original paragraph. As we do so, we will tell the reader what the four classifications are.

People traveling in states east of the Mississippi River soon realize that certain towns and cities on their itinerary have famous namesakes abroad. Representing *authors,* Georgia and Florida have a Milton, Illinois a Carlyle, New York a Homer and an Ovid, and Pennsylvania a Seneca. To dignify *explorers,* a Columbus is found in Georgia and Ohio, a De Soto and La Salle in Illinois, and a Ponce de León in Florida. In honor of *foreign statesmen,* a Bismarck appears in Illinois, a Napoleon in Michigan and Ohio, and an Elizabeth in Georgia, Illinois, New Jersey, Pennsylvania, and West Virginia. From prominent *centers of ancient culture,* Illinois includes Athens, Rome, Sparta, and Troy; New York has Athens, Babylon, Ithaca, Rome, and Troy. In fact, Troy appears in no fewer than eight states: Alabama, Indiana, Michigan, New Hampshire, North Carolina, Ohio, Pennsylvania, and Tennessee.

At this point we have achieved a unified and well-organized paragraph. Now let us look at another example of achieving unity through limitation. This time you decide to tell your reader in a paragraph about your favorite place to take a vacation. It would be dangerous to use this topic sentence:

The Caribbean is the best place to take a vacation.

There are hundreds of resort islands in the Caribbean Sea, and each has some unique feature. Perhaps you have a favorite, such as Martinique. Now, retaining your controlling idea, ". . . best place to take a vacation," you decide on this topic sentence:

Martinique, in the Caribbean, is the best place to take a vacation.

Having geographically limited your subject to something more manageable, you must now tell your reader *why* Martinique is the best place to take a vacation. At this point you will notice that the controlling idea also serves as a method of limitation. In jotting down reasons that will prove your point to your reader, you must test each to ensure that it is consistent with the controlling idea. Good shopping, a near-perfect climate, uncrowded beaches on warm, clear waters, friendly islanders, and enjoyable entertainment all meet the controlling-idea test. The fact that Martinique is a Department of France, or that its capital is Fort-de-France, does not meet the test.

Recognizing and Fixing the Controlling Idea

As we have seen, every paragraph, at least for now, should begin with a topic sentence that expresses the limited subject matter to be discussed in that paragraph. The controlling idea is the main part of the topic sentence. It is *the* idea about which the paragraph is to be written. It may be stated in a word, phrase, or clause.

Because the topic sentence, with its controlling idea, is a serviceable guide for achieving unity in the paragraph, you should place it first. Then, as you write, keep it clearly in mind. Allow it to control what you include and exclude. The topic sentence is your general frame of reference; the controlling idea is your specific focus.

Here is a list of topic sentences submitted by students; the language stating the controlling idea of each sentence is italicized. Analyze each to determine why the italicized elements represent the controlling ideas.

1. The house on Hominy Ridge was *haunted.*
2. Public service has a *special appeal* for some people.
3. Terrorism is a *dangerous threat to international security.*
4. The ordinary gas burner is a *simple mechanism.*
5. Our hopes of winning the championship depend on *whether our star quarterback, Joe Smith, will be eligible to play.*
6. *Save* me.
7. Save *me.*
8. The space program has been a *great expense* to this country.
9. The space program has been *an asset* to this country.
10. A winter in New England can be *very exciting.*

Failure to include a clearly defined controlling idea in a topic sentence will likely result in digressions and irrelevancies that can seriously weaken the effectiveness of a paragraph. Together, your topic sentence and controlling idea are your *commitment* to the reader. Be careful of making a promise you can't keep!

¶ Exercises

A. Write the controlling idea in each of the following topic sentences. Use as few words as possible.

1. Riot control requires some very special skills.
2. The space shuttle is really a small but sophisticated laboratory.
3. Hang gliding is a dangerous hobby.
4. A good dictionary is an indispensable tool of the writer.
5. During the holiday season, Boston Common is brilliantly lighted.
6. Summit meetings are successful only if the leaders there are willing to make substantial concessions.
7. He was always cheerful.
8. The ability to write a good paragraph is an acquired one.
9. We watched with awe as Mount St. Helens erupted again.
10. This may be the year that the Red Sox take the pennant.

B. Revise the following sentences so that each contains a *definite* controlling idea. Since you will have to limit each one somewhat, it will probably be necessary to change the meaning to some degree. Underline your controlling idea.

1. History is one of my favorite subjects.
2. John F. Kennedy was an outstanding leader.
3. Today a high school education is just not enough.
4. Most sporting events are very exciting.

C. Write three sentences of your own that are topic sentences with definite controlling ideas. Underline the controlling ideas in each.

Unified Support of the Controlling Idea

A well-developed paragraph depends on the writer's control of materials and procedure. Having developed an appropriately limited topic sentence, with its controlling idea, the writer must then develop the paragraph by explaining them. The explanation takes the form of supporting statements. Some statements are likely to be more important than others; *all* of them, however, must apply to the topic sentence that has been stated. More specifically, they must convince the reader by establishing the validity of the controlling idea with relation to the rest of the topic sentence. Any statement that does not fulfill this purpose will destroy the unity of the paragraph.

Major Support

Once you have a definite controlling idea clearly fixed in your mind, what is the next step? At this point, you should select from all you know about your subject such information as you need to support your controlling idea. In essence, testing each piece of information against the controlling idea is a sorting process. One good way to do this is to put the word *because* at the beginning of each sentence. Let us look at how this might be done.

Consider this topic sentence with the controlling idea in italics:

Charles "Speed" Jones was a *scheming politician*.

- *because:* At picnics near election time in Minisink County, he gave prospective voters and their children all the ice cream they could eat.
- *because:* He created opportunities to do favors for anyone who could control votes at the polling places.
- *because:* He used his office to introduce legislation that would favor his insurance and real estate business.
- *because:* He raised horses, and he was known to be kind to them.
- *because:* He was elected almost ten years ago.

Now you should notice two important things about this series of sentences. First, the initial three are unified with the controlling idea, *scheming politician*. The fourth sentence is definitely not unified, although it might be an excellent supporting sentence for another topic sentence such as, "Speed had another side, however—one of *compassionate caring."* The fifth sentence is confusing. One might take it to mean that *because* Speed is a scheming politician, he has managed to stay in office for ten years. But, as this case shows, the *because* test is really backwards, testing the controlling idea rather than the supporting sentence. Obviously, there are many politicians who do not scheme, yet stay in office far longer than Speed.

When you say that your controlling idea—"scheming politician"—is true "because . . ." and then give your evidence in one-two-three fashion, your sentences of explanation are likely to be definite supports of the controlling idea in your topic sentence. It follows that your series of sentences will be not only unified but, equally important, logical.

Try to think of unity as a flock of white sheep where you find unity of color, unity of kind, and unity of impression. If a wandering gray elephant were to stray into the flock, each of these unities would be weakened. Just one gray-elephant sentence in a paragraph breaks down the unity that your controlling idea leads the reader to expect.

The second important thing you should note about the "Charles Jones" sentences above is the function of the *because* statements as *support of the controlling idea.* As readers, we may assume from the first three in the series of sentences given us by the writer that the three ideas—namely, the one about "ice cream," the one about "favors," and the one about "the insurance and real estate business"—were the most important ideas that the writer wanted to use at the time. These three ideas, therefore, are the *major* supporting statements, designed to convince the reader of the validity of the controlling idea.

Of course, in composing a paragraph you do not write the word *because* at the beginning of each sentence. You should, however, *think* the *because* before you express your sentence-idea. The *because* test is a way to help you fix your attention upon the specific focus you have chosen for the subject area of your topic sentence. By establishing the validity of your controlling idea, you will probably convince your readers; by distorting your focus you will only confuse them. In most paragraphs *because* will serve your purposes very well. On occasion you may prefer to substitute *for instance,* or *specifically,* or *namely,* or some similar test word. The important point is this: whether you use *because* or a substitute, *test each sentence-idea* to be used in the paragraph *with the same test word.*

Sometimes a controlling idea requires a specific number of supporting statements. In the "Charles Jones" topic sentence the controlling idea did not imply a particular number of "proofs" for the validity of the topic sentence.

The writer settled on three; he or she might have given ten. But in the following example, the controlling idea calls for *three* effects, and three must be expressed.

The treaty of Versailles had *three outstanding effects.*

- *because:* First, a League of Nations was formed.
- *because:* Second, a reduction of German armaments relieved the whole world from threatened German aggression.
- *because:* Third, German colonies were awarded to various nations.

Notice that each of the three sentences serves as a *because* (or "namely") statement in direct support of the controlling idea with reference to "The Treaty of Versailles." And since the controlling idea, in this particular sentence, mentions *three* effects, the writer has given three, not two or five. *A topic sentence with its controlling idea, once expressed, obligates the writer to fulfill a given task, and a paragraph is not successfully composed until that obligation is met.*

Paragraphs with Major Support Only

In many of the paragraphs you write, you will be able to develop your controlling idea adequately with a series of statements or examples that do not require further explanation or proof. In the following example, the writer backs up the statement in her topic sentence by giving specific facts in support of it.

No leader of the Revolution except George Washington had a more difficult task than the Governor of New Jersey. The state was split almost fifty-fifty between Loyalists and rebels. Morale was a constant problem. Thousands gave up the fight and signed secret agreements with the British to remain neutral in return for a "protection." Others took advantage of the chaos to loot and abuse their neighbors. Still others concentrated on getting rich. In the middle of the war, [Governor] Livingston wrote to Washington: "I am so discouraged by our public mismanagement that I almost sink under it." [1]*

MARGARET TRUMAN *Women of Courage*

*Numbers within parentheses refer to the listing of complete source information appearing on pages 199–203.

Writing about the habitat of birds, this next author turned his observations into illustrations of the antics of the chickadee.

> Storms with high winds that upset the equilibrium of other birds do not upset chickadees. People out in the rain see the acrobatic chickadee always headed into the wind to prevent rain or snow from being blown under his feathers from behind. In winter, when other birds have taken refuge, he comes out of his nesting hole in the trunk and frolics in a snowstorm. He will zip over to a dripping icicle and, without any support except for the sensitive mechanism of wings and tail, catch the drops as they fall off the end of the icicle more neatly than you or I can drink from a fountain. [2]

> RUTHERFORD PLATT   *The River of Life*

Often a person's character can be highlighted by a story about one of his or her special weaknesses. Here, in a single illustration made up of nine sentences, the author reveals the poet Tennyson's vanity.

> Tennyson, while affecting to dread observation, was none the less no little vain, a weakness of which Meredith gave this amusing illustration. Tennyson and William Morris were once walking together on a road in the Isle of Wight. Suddenly in the distance appeared two cyclists wheeling toward them. Tennyson immediately took alarm and growled out, "Oh, Morris, what shall I do? Those fellows are sure to bother me!" Thereupon Morris said, "I'll see that they don't bother you." The cyclists came on, sped by without a sign, and presently disappeared on the horizon. There was a moment or two of silence, and then Tennyson, evidently huffed that he had attracted no attention, once more growled out, "They never even looked at me." [3]

> RICHARD LE GALLIENNE   *The Romantic 90's*

The following paragraph contains the striking details of what must have been a striking event. Notice that they are presented as evidence that the spectators could not "keep back gasps of admiration," as stated in the topic sentence.

> So gorgeous was the spectacle on the May morning of 1910 when nine kings rode in the funeral of Edward VII of England that the crowd,

waiting in hushed and black-clad awe, could not keep back gasps of admiration. In scarlet and blue and green and purple, three by three the sovereigns rode through the palace gates, with plumed helmets, gold braid, crimson sashes, and jeweled orders flashing in the sun. After them came five heirs apparent, forty more imperial or royal highnesses, seven queens—four dowager and three regnant—and a scattering of special ambassadors from uncrowned countries. Together they represented seventy nations in the greatest assemblage of royalty and rank ever gathered in one place. The muffled tongue of Big Ben tolled nine by the clock as the cortege left the palace, but on history's clock it was sunset, and the sun of the old world was setting in a dying blaze of splendor never to be seen again. [4]

BARBARA W. TUCHMAN   *The Guns of August*

Minor Support

In the preceding paragraphs, only major supporting sentences are needed. The topic sentence with its controlling idea is developed by one sentence after another, each serving as individual support. Even when illustrations are used—which may take more than one sentence—the illustration as a unit is treated as an individual support of the controlling idea. Good paragraphs, as we have seen, can be written with major supporting statements only.

However, a sentence containing facts, examples, or other evidence that clarifies or explains the meaning of a major supporting statement is called a *minor supporting statement*. Let us look at an example of how a minor supporting statement might be developed in support of a major one.

Suppose that you have developed the following topic sentence:

In the early 1970s, many public schools faced doubtful survival.

Your major supporting statements might be

- *because:* Financial funds to maintain services were inadequate.
- *because:* In many instances the level of instruction was dangerously lowered.

Both are good major supporting sentences because they support the controlling idea, *doubtful survival.* The problem is, however, that your reader might well wonder *why* funds were inadequate or *why* the level of instruction was lowered. To put it another way, these two major supporting statements are vague and therefore need some explanation. And that is the purpose of the minor supporting statement. It supports the major supporting statement, which, in turn, supports the controlling idea.

Now you must address a reader's reasonable question—"Why?"—before he or she gets the chance to ask it. Again, the *because* test is a fitting one in answer to the question, Why? *Why* were financial funds to maintain services inadequate?

- • *because:* Voters repeatedly rejected levies to provide money for teachers' salaries and basic maintenance.
- • *because:* National and state austerity programs cut off the normal funds they had been providing.

Why was the level of instruction lowered?

- • *because:* Many teachers quit or went on strike over salary disputes.
- • *because:* Teaching loads became so high that the quality of instruction was consequently impaired.

Each of the two major statements gives a good reason for accepting the controlling idea. In turn, each major supporting sentence has two minor supporting sentences. The *because* test has been applied to each of the major statements and each of the minor statements. *All* statements therefore support the controlling idea. Now, if you remove the word *because* from each sentence and write the sentences, one after the other, in paragraph form, you will have a unified paragraph. And that is just what is wanted!

The present discussion is about paragraph unity. There may be times, simply as a matter of style, that you will want to combine two or more minor supporting statements or sentences into one. We will discuss style later. Still, it is a good idea for you, as you organize your paragraph, to follow the process described above.

And a very important word of caution! All too often writers carelessly admit into a paragraph something that looks like a *minor* supporting statement but is irrelevant. For example, a minor supporting statement such as "Voters attended meetings held by school boards and expressed dissatisfaction with the way schools were being run," would not survive the *because* test. Voters might well do so in times of very adequate funding. Criticism is simply not the threat that inadequate funding is.

When you prepare to write a paragraph and are in the organizational stage, you must decide whether the controlling idea can be supported with only a series of major statements, or whether it requires minor supporting statements as well. The key to your decision will usually lie in the major supporting statements themselves. As we saw, two perfectly good major statements were vague enough to need further clarification. But say you find yourself in a course facing the examination questions, "What were the chief political causes of the French Revolution?" In answering the question, you might well rely on several major statements. But if your instructor has added the words "discuss," "analyze," or "explain," you should be warned that minor support will be needed.

The Relation of Major and Minor Support

Here is a three-part rule to follow as you develop a paragraph that begins with a definite controlling idea:

1. *Every* major supporting statement in the paragraph should be a direct and definite explanation of the controlling idea stated in the topic sentence.

2. *Every* minor supporting statement should explain its major statement *in terms of the controlling idea.*

3. Exam questions involving *discuss, explain,* or *analyze* usually require both major and minor supporting material.

¶ Exercises

A. Under the heading "major support," list from the following paragraph the numbers of those sentences that serve as major supporting statements; under "minor support," do the same for those used as minor supporting statements. Note that the topic sentence is not numbered. It would be a good idea before you start your lists to identify the controlling idea.

The Treaty of Versailles had three important effects.¹First, a League of Nations was formed. ²By uniting, the member nations would keep peace among themselves and would aid one another if an attack came from an outside enemy. [3]Submitting their own disputes to the League Council for arbitration would reduce the possibility of armed conflict. [4]Second, the reduction of German military strength relieved the whole world of the threat of German aggression. [5]Commissions of control, appointed by the Allies, entered Germany and supervised the execution of the disarmament clauses of the treaty. [6]The Allies destroyed great stores of armaments, munitions, and war supplies and sent investigating teams into areas suspected of hiding or manufacturing such materials. [7]The Allies also dismantled the German navy with the exception of a few ships and set about reducing naval personnel to 15,000 men. [8]Third, German colonies became the spoils of various nations. [9]Her African holdings went to France and Great Britain. [10]Shantung, China, which Germany had seized, became a prize of Japan.

B. The following sentences are taken in order from a paragraph that discusses three important effects of a shopping mall that has been opened just outside the limits of a city. The topic sentence is stated first; then each sentence-idea is listed and numbered. Number your paper from 1 to 11 and, for each, write *because* if it is a valid major or minor statement and X if it violates the unity of the paragraph.

TOPIC SENTENCE: A new shopping mall, just outside the city limits, has three definite effects on the urban community.

1. First, it has a novelty that attracts not only shoppers but also the curious.

2. People just enjoy visiting the colorful, modern shops that line the indoor concourse.

3. Seventy stores with their great variety of merchandise are easily and quickly accessible to all.

4. Downtown banks have branches in the mall to serve regular customers.

5. Second, a new mall siphons off business from inner city stores.

6. Large stores like Sears and Penney's often move from the downtown area to a new mall, luring customers with enlarged floor space and increased stocks and services.

7. Many shoe stores, dress shops, boutiques, and gift shops under one roof give shoppers wider choices in shorter time, no matter what the weather.

8. With careful planning, a stepped-up program of reconstruction, and modern landscaping, the inner cities in most communities could revive consumer interest.

9. Third, the mall, being located outside of the city limits, deprives the city of much-needed revenues.

10. Sizable property taxes on the huge complex go to the county in which it is located.

11. People who work in the stores and offices, and in related services in the mall, pay no city income tax.

C. In this exercise only the topic sentence and the major supporting statements from an original paragraph are supplied. It is up to you to compose two minor supporting statements for each.

TOPIC SENTENCE: In the course of a day, students do far more than just attend classes.

MAJOR SUPPORT: In order to maintain their health, they must exercise.

1. _____
2. _____

MAJOR SUPPORT: Because much of what they learn in a course is not provided in the classroom, they must do research in the library.

1. _____
2. _____

MAJOR SUPPORT: Finally, for the education beyond books, they participate in cultural and social activities.

1. _____
2. _____

D. Write a topic sentence with a definite controlling idea. Underline the controlling idea. Write three major supporting statements; then write two minor supporting statements for each major one.

Paragraph Unity and the Controlling Idea

Here are two paragraphs analyzed according to the principles we have been discussing. One is by a student, the other by a professional writer. The sentences in the student's paragraph are numbered for the purpose of analysis.

A Student's Paragraph

NATURAL BEAUTIES OF AMERICA

The national parks of America are havens of supreme beauty. ¹Thousands of miles of roads and trails serve over 125 million people annually. ²Yosemite Falls, the loftiest in America, plunges 2,500 feet with such force that the earth trembles and thunder fills the valley. ³In Sequoia Park the Four Guardsmen finger the sky, members of coast redwoods that achieve girths of 44 feet and heights of over 360 feet. ⁴Preparing the parks to accommodate their visitors has cost the government a billion dollars. ⁵From the rim of the Grand Canyon, one looks down 1,500 feet into the Colorado River gorge cut from primordial rock a billion and a half years old. ⁶Back from the rim is the Canyon Village complex, built at a cost of eight million dollars, to provide food, lodgings, and services. ⁷Inspiring awe are such flowers as the beavertail cactus in California's Death Valley, asters on Mr. Rainier, and the yellow lady's-slipper and deep-pink mountain laurel on the slopes of the Great Smokies. ⁸In the presence of such beauty, it is a shame that thoughtless, careless tourists pollute the roads, streams, and picnic areas with paper cups and plates and old beer cans!

This paragraph clearly lacks unity. To discover why, let us go over it sentence by sentence looking for ideas that lead away from the main idea stated in the topic sentence.

Obviously, the controlling idea of this paragraph is *havens of supreme beauty.* Once the writer has stated this, he or she must give examples of supreme beauty preserved in these sheltered areas. Anything else does not belong.

In the first sentence, we find the writer straying from the point: the thousands of miles of trails and roads are a necessary convenience to visitors, but they are not of themselves things of supreme beauty. Sentences 2 and 3 adequately support the controlling idea, but sentence 4 does not. Like sentence 1, this one concerns services that make natural beauties available to tourists, but it does nothing to support the controlling idea. Dollars and cents have little to do with beauty! Sentence 5 is fine, but sentence 6 is hardly about natural beauty. It might as well read "pizza parlors, motels, and gas stations."

In sentence 7, the mention of wildflowers is very much in keeping with the controlling idea. Sentence 8 is merely the opinion of the writer. He or she is entitled to it, but it has no place in this particular paragraph. Thus, of the eight numbered sentences, 2, 3, 5, and 7 develop the controlling idea. The others do not.

When working with details, facts, or examples, you may prefer to use *for instance* instead of *because.* The test confirms the unity of these sentences:

The national parks of America are havens of supreme beauty.

- *for instance:* Yosemite Falls, the loftiest in America . . .
- *for instance:* In Sequoia Park the Four Guardsmen . . .
- *for instance:* From the rim of the Grand Canyon . . .
- *for instance:* Inspiring awe are such flowers . . .

But the test rules out sentences 1, 4, 6, and 8:

The national parks of America are havens of supreme beauty.

- *for instance:* Thousands of miles of roads . . .
- *for instance:* Preparing the parks to accommodate . . .
- *for instance:* Back from the rim is the Canyon Village Complex . . .
- *for instance:* In the presence of such beauty it is a shame . . .

Having eliminated the sentences that do not belong in the paragraph, we have left the writer with only about half of the original material. More important, what is left is unified and clearly supports the controlling idea. At this point, the writer could add additional supporting materials. Before (*not* after) doing so, however, he or she should test them with *because* or *for instance.*

Here is a revision of the paragraph as it might be rewritten in the light of the foregoing suggestions:

> The national parks of America are havens of supreme beauty. Yosemite Falls, the loftiest in America, plunges 2,500 feet with such force that the earth trembles and thunder fills the valley. In Bryce Canyon, Utah, multicolored rock spikes resemble terraced Rhine castles, Moslem minarets, and cathedral towers dropped all together, right-side up, to fill in part of one yawning chasm in the Rockies. In Sequoia the Four Guardsmen finger the sky, members of coast redwoods that achieve girths of 44 feet and heights over 360 feet. One can stand on the rim of the Grand Canyon and look down 1,500 feet into the Colorado River gorge cut from primordial rock a billion and a half years old. The Everglades of southern Florida teem with dazzling beauty. Here there are snowy egrets and blazing spoonbills, eagles and hundreds of other wild birds, the fascinating colors of reptiles and swamp life, the long, low reaches of swampland stretching out to meet the sun. Inspiring awe are such flowers as the beavertail cactus in the Death Valley of California, asters on Mt. Rainier, yellow lady's-slipper and deep-pink mountain laurel on the slopes of the Great Smokies. Jean Pierre, the famous Alpinist, once remarked, "In so many places America offers her people preeminent loveliness."

A Professional Writer's Paragraph

The second paragraph for analysis is from an article in a leading magazine. It illustrates the type you might write for a teacher of geography or social science. The author is discussing Montana as a "treasure state"; that is, a state full of treasures. As you read it, carefully apply the *because* test to each sentence after the topic sentence.

The Commonwealth that was lawless wilderness eighty-five years ago is aptly nicknamed the "Treasure State." Beneath its mountains still lies untold mineral wealth, though its mines have already disgorged billions of dollars. Its farms, both nonirrigated and irrigated, produce stupendous yields of wheat, hay, sugar beets, and other crops. Over its grassy hills and plains range thousands of fine cattle, sheep, horses, and hogs. Agriculture has gone far ahead of even mining in money income. From 25 million acres of forest, lumbermen reap rich harvests. Oil, now produced in many fields, is a source of profit rapidly attaining major development, and natural gas is plentiful in much of the State. In numerous rushing rivers roars unlimited water power. [5]

Leo A. Borah   "Montana"

Here the author's major support lies in three types of treasure: minerals, agriculture, and energy sources. Each of his sentences clearly meets the *because* test. It is therefore unified. But suppose the author had included this sentence: "An art museum in Butte contains art treasures painted by European masters." Very obviously this statement is not in unity with the rest of the paragraph.

The Compound Controlling Idea

A topic sentence, if the subject matter requires it, may have a compound controlling idea. That is, the central thought of the paragraph may have two (or more) parts, each of which must be developed. For example:

- On the battle field of Waterloo, Wellington's infantry faced two major horrors—*cavalry* and *artillery.*
- A man owes it to himself to have a *modest checking account,* a *few friends,* and *integrity.*
- American scientists have developed methods of firing missiles *from land bases* and *from submarines at sea.*
- Fred pronounced himself to be *ready, willing,* and *able* to work.

For full development, topic sentences such as these may require more than a single paragraph; perhaps a paragraph for each part of the controlling idea.

However, on occasion, if the writer's material is limited or if only a superficial treatment is asked for, a single paragraph will be sufficient.

A single paragraph developing a compound controlling idea requires that each part of the compound be explained according to the principles we have already discussed in the development of a single controlling idea. The first topic sentence above could probably be adequately handled in a single paragraph. Let us look at each of the two parts of the compound controlling idea. First, we must ask the question, *"Why* would cavalry be a horror to infantry?"* Then, having asked *why,* we can answer *because.* As a major supporting statement, we might say *because* a foot soldier is at a severe disadvantage when facing a mounted enemy. Then we might develop minor statements that, first, the mounted soldier has the advantage of height and, second, speed. And then, what about artillery? *Because* the infantryman's rifle is simply no match for the artilleryman's cannon. Minor support might include the fact that the fire of artillery weapons can be massed for a devastating effect and that the radius of destruction of artillery fire is many times greater than that of small arms.

Let us now look at some examples of paragraphs developed to support topic sentences with two or more controlling ideas. The first gives the writer's reasons for the rapid growth of machine-assisted work in three areas of American life.

Automatic machinery in recent years has revolutionized the operation of the office, the factory, and even the classroom. In addition to the simple electric typewriters and mimeographing machines, the photo-duplicators and complex computers make office work a paradise for harried managers and supervisors and for overworked secretarial staff. Automated office equipment expedites all types of paper work, such as recording, analyzing, filing, and estimating, and does the work more accurately and more economically. In the factory the large-scale use of automatic equipment is responsible for the great strides made by the electronics industry. Without mechanization the total labor force available to specialized industry today could not produce the great volume of goods needed by the public, commerce, industry, and the armed services. Finally, in the classroom, machines have hastened the learning process in limited areas. Television sets, film projectors, phonographs, and tape recorders make lectures and demonstrations possible in the huge classes of today's colleges and universities. Even in small schools, where enrollments are limited, these same audio-visual aids, when they are properly controlled, allow individual students to learn materials at their own rate of speed, with the result that the slow learner does not hold back the student who has greater potential for growth.

The following paragraph by George Santayana, a Spanish philosopher who wrote in English, is developed from a compound controlling idea through the use of reasons, two of which are supported by an indirect form of illustration.

Poets may be divided into two classes: the musicians and the psychologists. The first are masters of significant language as harmony; they know what notes to sound together and in succession; they can produce, by the marshalling of sounds and images, by the fugue of passion and the snap of wit, a thousand brilliant effects out of old materials. The Ciceronian orator, the epigrammatic, lyric, and elegiac poets give examples of this art. The psychologists, on the other hand, gain their effect not by the intrinsic mastery of language, but by the closer adaptation of it to things. The dramatic poets naturally furnish an illustration. [6]

The Sense of Beauty

Our final paragraph has a compound controlling idea supported by illustrations. Here each of them, consisting of more than one sentence, forms a unit, and it is *as a unit* that the illustration maintains its unity with the controlling idea. Thus, each illustration is like one major support. Although there are no minor supporting statements in this paragraph, there could have been.

The deaths of three contemporary English poets—Keats, Shelley, and Byron—had about them a touch of irony. John Keats, suffering from tuberculosis, went to the warm climate of southern Italy to recuperate so that he might return to England and marry Fanny Brawne. He died in Rome a few months later and lies buried in the Protestant Cemetery near the tomb of Caius Cestus. Shelley, too, left England for Italy to recover his health and to write poems that would bring him fame in his homeland. There, while enjoying one of his favorite pastimes, sailing, he was drowned in the Gulf of Spezia during a sudden squall. Though Shelley, while in England, had attempted to draw close to Keats and had been unsuccessful, his body was also buried in the Protestant Cemetery in Rome, just a few yards from the grave of Keats. Lord Byron, on the other hand, left England with the full intention of never returning, and died at

Missolonghi in the Greek fight for freedom. Despite the efforts of Greek patriots to have him entombed in Greece, his friends had his body returned to England and buried it at Hucknall Torkard, not far from Newstead Abbey, his boyhood home.

In each of these three paragraphs, the controlling idea has been supported by examples. Another type of compound controlling idea involves development by means of comparison or contrast. These topic sentences are examples:

- Byron and Hemingway both found themselves famous at twenty-five.
- The great differences between the civilizations of Greece and China were due largely to the fact that the Greeks were impulsive and the Chinese were cautious.

The uses of comparison and contrast, along with other complex methods, are considered in Chapter 6.

Basic Principles of Paragraph Unity: A Summary

Unity is essential to good paragraph writing. It calls for clear thinking and a definite plan of organization. You begin with a controlling idea and develop a topic sentence as a vehicle for it. Next you develop your major supports for the controlling idea. Each must relate back to the controlling idea. In some situations you might want to develop minor supporting statements that further explain your major supporting statements. Applying the test word *because* properly and appropriately throughout the paragraph is one sure way of achieving unity. If the topic sentence has a compound controlling idea, you must develop each part according to the principles of unity.

¶ Exercises

A. Copy the topic sentence and then list the numbers identifying the accompanying statements. After each number tell whether its statement is (1) "in unity" or (2) "not in unity" with the controlling idea. Judge each sentence-idea by itself, but remember the function of minor supporting statements.

Topic Sentence: Automobile racing is an expensive sport.

1. Le Mans and the Indianapolis Speedway are famous for their races.
2. Successful drivers demand and get large sums of money.
3. Just the engine for a racing car may cost hundreds of thousands of dollars.
4. Drivers and tracks both get international publicity.
5. The crew to support just one racing car may have up to ten members.
6. Many people, both drivers and spectators, lose their lives annually.
7. They attract the very best international drivers and cars.
8. Personnel to operate, direct, and maintain race courses involve a major financial investment.
9. Advertising racing events in the mass media takes huge sums of money.
10. Maintenance costs of equipment often exceed original costs.
11. A good pit crew can refuel a car and change a bad tire in a matter of seconds.

B. For each of the following paragraphs, copy the topic sentence with its identifying number and underline the controlling idea. Then, below, list the numbers of those sentences that are *not* in unity with the controlling idea. Be sure you consider all minor supporting statements that belong in the paragraph. If a large number of sentences are out of unity, explain why.

1. What it takes for a pleasant vacation you can find in and near our cabin in the semiwilds of Canada, northeast of Sault Ste. Marie. [1]There are peace and quiet, which you can't buy in the city. [2]Some people can sleep with a thousand car horns coughing raucously in the night. [3]The telephone company has not discovered our isolated cabin as yet, so there are no calls to bother us. [4]The rates for telephone service would probably be exorbitant, anyway. [5]Besides, it's fun to get away from civilization for a while. [6]Our lake is just right for the anglers. [7]The bass and the pike are the biggest, fastest, tastiest, and scrappiest to be found anywhere. [8]And when the day is done and the supper things are put away, the fireplace, piled up with sweet-smelling logs, provides just the kind of natural tranquilizer a person needs to sleep well under about three double blankets.

2. The sciences and the arts have flourished together. [1]They have been fixed together as sharply in place as in time. [2]In some way both spring from one civilization: the civilization of the Mediterranean, which expresses itself in action. [3]There are civilizations which have a different outlook; they express themselves in contemplation, and in them neither science nor the arts are practiced as such. [4]For a civilization which expresses itself in contemplation values no creative activity. [5]What it values is a mystic immersion in nature, the union with what already exists. [7]

J. BRONOWSKI   "The Creative Process"

3. Even at this early date, it seems probable that for certain kinds of instruction TV works as well as live teaching. [1]This, of course, may be less proof of the value of TV than of the failure or misdirection of much conventional teaching. [2]The acquisition of factual knowledge may not be what the student should get in class. [3]Too often the American student uses the classroom as a substitute for study. [4]If the classroom has such a function, it is the place for testing ideas and skills, and for the interchange of ideas. [8]

ERNEST EARNEST   "Must the TV Technicians Take Over the Colleges?"

4. Throughout his career as a judge and mayor, Gaynor kept his private life strictly to himself. [1]Few people knew that he had been born on a farm, that he had once studied for the priesthood, or that he had been married twice. [2]Photographs of his wife and children were non-existent as far as the public was concerned. [3]He went home every weekend to a farm on Long Island, at St. James, and tolerated no intrusion except for neighboring farmers with whom he would discuss crops, weather conditions, and purely local affairs. [4]He was a political and mental giant among pygmies. [5]Compared to Gaynor, Jimmy Walker was a department store floorwalker; LaGuardia, an opportunist whom Gaynor would have given the back of his hand; and Impellitteri would have done well to have been allowed to tie Gaynor's shoelaces. [6]About LaGuardia, I can never forgive him for having withheld the salary of Professor Bertrand Russell when the mob was hounding the British philosopher out of the City College of New York for teaching "advanced" ideas. [7]One may well wonder what Gaynor would have done in this case. [8]He probably

would have delivered Russell's pay envelope himself, and with his cane carved a path through the mob of shouting obscurantists. [9]

HARRY GOLDEN   *Only in America*

5. The size of the dog you buy should be determined by the size of your home and its location. [1]A big dog needs a lot of space just to walk around. [2]Generally, he also needs more exercise. [3]If he cannot get his exercise unescorted, and you are a conscientious dog owner, you will have to exercise along with him. [4]However good this might be for you, you may find it's more exercise than you want. [5]A large dog, too, will need more food, and the difference in cost may be noticeable in the household budget. [6]An average-size dog eats about $20 worth of dog food a month. [10]

Consumer Reports, XXIV

C. Each of the following paragraphs lacks a topic sentence and controlling idea. Read each one carefully and determine from the supporting sentences what central idea is developed. Then copy the number of the paragraph and write a topic sentence with an appropriate controlling idea.

1. He would insult a man who disagreed with him about the weather. He would pull endless wires in order to meet some man who admired his work, and was able and anxious to be of use to him—and would proceed to make a mortal enemy of him with some idiotic and wholly uncalled-for exhibition of arrogance and bad manners. A character in one of his operas was a caricature of one of the most powerful music critics of his day. Not content with burlesquing him, he invited the critic to his house and read the libretto aloud in front of his friends. [11]

DEEMS TAYLOR   *Of Men and Music*

2. One aim is that the Russians perceive an opportunity to score a propaganda triumph through asserting in a dramatic top-level conference their claim to be peace-loving. Another is that Russia wants a drop in interna-

tional tensions both as a means of slowing up Western defense efforts and to concentrate on its own economic problems. [12]

New York Times

3. Examples of higher status symbols are push-button controlled draperies, "His and Her" bathrooms, and television sets installed in bedroom ceilings. One highly successful builder northwest of Chicago showed me a gold-plated faucet in the guest bathroom of one of his houses. He said that this feature had proved to be so popular that he is introducing it as an optional accessory in his $40,000 houses. The gold faucet, he explained, is "a little $500 extra" that not only impresses the neighbors, but also adds to the resale value of the house. [13]

VANCE PACKARD   "The Pursuit of Status"

D. Write a paragraph using only major supporting statements on one of the following topics. Limit the topic so that it can be discussed in a paragraph of about 150 to 200 words. Carefully formulate your topic sentence and make your controlling idea clear and definite.

1. What a hobby should be
2. What a satisfying career should be
3. Life in a computer memory bank
4. The ethics of some people in business aren't what they might be.
5. The several achievements of Martin Luther King
6. What is it the Soviets really want?
7. Three ways to fight pollution
8. College athletes should be held to an academic standard.
9. The study of philosophy can be pretty dull at times.
10. The call for excellence in American education isn't being heeded.

2.
Basic Materials of Paragraph Development

As we noted in Chapter 1, the topic sentence, together with its controlling idea, is really a promise to the reader. And that reader will expect you to fulfill your promise. There are a number of ways to do so, but basically you will want to give your reader details, reasons, or illustrations and examples. Your task is similar to that of a lawyer in court. It is not enough for the district attorney to say that John Smith robbed a bank. The prosecution must *prove* it with facts called evidence.

Once you have stated your topic sentence, you will need to consider the evidence most appropriate in developing it. Although you may mix types of support, you have the choice of using details, reasons, and illustrations or examples. It is possible that your reader may not even be aware of the type of support you are using, but you should be very much aware of it. Your topic sentence will usually lead to the selection of one type or another. In the following paragraphs, all about diamonds, notice how the topic sentence and particularly the controlling idea suggest a type of support.

DETAIL

Few people know the basic facts about diamonds. They consist of pure crystallized carbon and are usually found in the form of crystals. They come in many shapes: some have eight facets; others have forty-eight. Diamonds are the hardest substance known, and for this reason acids do not affect them. They are, however, brittle and can be split. To polish diamonds one must use oil and diamond powder.

REASON

People who own diamonds often think of them as one measure of prestige. A number of large blue-white stones suggest a certain affluence. A really valuable necklace or tiara gives its owner not only evidence of wealth but also a sense of superiority, whether it is merited or not. And although many people buy diamonds as an investment, they can display the investment with more effect than stock certificates or bank books.

ILLUSTRATION OR EXAMPLE

Diamonds have lured many people into trouble. The famous Nikolas Verden stole the Khybar stone from a shop in Amsterdam, Holland, fled to Naples, and died trying to escape the police. Thomas Bright, a jewelry salesman, swallowed the Van Noos diamond in order to smuggle it out of South Africa and was arrested after it was found during an operation for appendicitis. Five members of the Burton family died trying to hide the Courtney stone from the authorities.

In the first example, the writer used the words "basic facts," which was a commitment to supply them. In the second example the writer expressed an opinion, although it was that of others. Opinions are often best explained with reasons. In the third example, illustrations appear to be appropriate for the topic sentence.

Details, which are facts or at least factual in nature, come from reading, observation, analysis, conversation, and other sources of experience and knowledge. There will be times when you will need more details than you have at hand, and you will have to consult reference works or other literary sources to find additional ones. *Reasons* are ideas formed in the mind by logical thinking; that is, they are the result of deductive or inductive thinking. Both are systems of logic suited to two different purposes. Deduction involves concluding specific facts from a general statement. Induction, on the other hand, involves an examination of facts and, from them, coming to a general conclusion. Opinions are best supported by reasons.

Illustrations or *examples* may be thought of as anecdotes or incidents from almost any area of experience that you have had, that another has had, or from your inventiveness as a writer. It is as if the writer has made a statement and then says, "Here, let me show you." At times, of course, words are inadequate to illustrate something and a picture must be used.

Paragraphs using *details* to support a topic sentence might include the specific features of a person's appearance, factual items concerning a devastating tornado, the requirements for American citizenship, the economic effects of a tax increase, the objectives of a political movement, or other matters.

On the other hand, a paragraph developed by *reasons* would include the writer's thoughts on a given topic. If, for example, you are of the opinion that freedom is worth fighting for, you must give reasons for your opinion; otherwise, it is bare opinion and not worth much except to you.

Finally, a paragraph using *illustration* or *example* as supporting material would be developed by means of one or more anecdotes or incidents written in such a way that the reader experiences a sense of action—something happening, if you will—that is stated or implied. Consider this short paragraph: "Mr. Atkins is certainly thrifty. When he buys a new automobile, he visits all of the dealers looking for the best buy. Periodically he checks the interest rates at all the banks in town and moves his account to get the highest one. Why, he even clips coupons from the newspaper to get a better price on the food he buys for his dog." If each of the three illustrations or examples in this paragraph is true, the point that Mr. Atkins is thrifty is well taken.

Let us now examine each type of basic material used to support a topic sentence and controlling idea and consider samples written by students and professional writers.

Detail

A paragraph supported with details is really one that is supported by facts or material factual in nature. There are essentially two kinds of details. There are those facts that are perceived by your five physical senses and, as far as you are concerned, are verifiable for that reason alone. For example, after a storm you notice that a fence has been blown away. That fact is a detail that would help support a topic sentence such as, "The storm last night must have been one of the worst in recent years." Other sensory perceptions that you might have had could have come from hearing the howling of the wind or feeling the beat of the heavy rain on your face.

The other kind of details are those that make up directions and procedures. They are conceptual in nature but expressed as facts. If, for example, you are writing a paragraph about driving on icy roads, you might warn your reader not to brake suddenly. It is a detail but not a fact, although it is *expressed* as a fact. A good test for each detail is the word *specifically,* just as the word *because* was a good test for unity. When you are driving on icy roads, there are specific things that should be done, and some that should not be done.

Often there will be times when you will have to rely on the perceptions of others for your facts and details. When you do, it is important that you get them from sources that are reliable.

The following paragraphs illustrate the use of detail in support of topic sentences and controlling ideas. The first, which is a somewhat more detailed version of the example on page 30, might be the result of a research assignment.

> Few people know the basic facts about diamonds. They consist of pure crystallized carbon and are usually found in the form of crystals. They come in many different shapes: some have eight facets; others have forty-eight. Diamonds are the hardest substance known, and for this reason acids do not affect them. They are, however, brittle and can be split. To polish diamonds one must use oil and diamond powder. Purity of color is rare in a diamond; most stones are cloudy, owing to small grooves or air bubbles. Diamonds are found in many parts of the world: for example, in India, China, Malaysia, Australia, Africa, Brazil, and even in the United States. The huge Cullinan diamond weighed 3025 carats. The largest and most perfect of the blue-stone diamonds, known as the Hope diamond, is worth a very great fortune.

This paragraph contains a wealth of details about diamonds. You might ask yourself how many of them you knew before reading the paragraph. Now, having read it, you know some basic facts about diamonds. The purpose of the paragraph has been achieved.

The next paragraph is interesting not only as an example of how details can support a controlling idea, but also of how vivid such details can be. The author of the analysis of faces drew from his experiences among the migrant agricultural workers in California. In a federal camp for these transient laborers, he became interested in the faces about him and what it was that lay behind them. Each kind of face he identifies is a vivifying detail of the "face-consciousness" that resulted from his close observation of the human beings with whom he lived and worked.

I began evaluating my fellow tramps as human material, and for the first time in my life I became face-conscious. There were good faces, particularly among the young. Several of the middle-aged and the old looked healthy and well preserved. But the damaged and decayed faces were in the majority. I saw faces that were wrinkled, or bloated, or raw as the surface of a peeled plum. Some of the noses were purple and swollen, some broken, some pitted with enlarged pores. There were many toothless mouths (I counted seventy-eight). I noticed eyes that were blurred, faded, opaque, or bloodshot. I was struck by the fact that the old men, even the very old, showed their age mainly in the face. [14]

ERIC HOFFER   "The Role of the Undesirables"

This paragraph is obviously based on the author's observations, which became facts to him.

The next paragraph also contains vivid details that lead to a feeling of sadness for the destruction of animal life caused by chemical spraying.

As the chemical penetrated the soil, the poisoned beetle grubs crawled out on the ground where they remained for some time before they died, attractive to insect-eating birds. Dead and dying insects of various species were conspicuous for about two weeks after the treatment. The effect on the bird populations could easily have been foretold. Brown thrashers, starlings, meadowlarks, grackles, and pheasants were virtually wiped out. Robins were "almost annihilated," according to the biologists' report. Dead earthworms had been seen in numbers after a gentle rain; probably the robins had fed on the poisoned worms. For other birds, too, the once beneficial rain had been changed, through the evil power of the poison introduced into their world, into an agent of destruction. Birds seen drinking and bathing in puddles left by rain a few days after the sprayings were inevitably doomed. [15]

RACHEL CARSON   *The Silent Spring*

How would you go about describing a city you know well? Probably the most effective way to suggest the special quality of a place is through the accumulation of specific details. In the paragraph that follows, the writer uses details to suggest what the *new* metropolis of New York was like.

As the second half of the nineteenth century began, New York became a metropolis. The "Empire City," strangers called it. They were awed by the splendor of its hotels and theaters and its costly, magnificent stores. They were astonished by the incessant torrent of traffic, the day-long, night-long surge and roar of more than five hundred thousand people. To many of them, New York seemed a city of crowds and carnival—breezy, recklessly extravagant, perpetually bent on pleasure. The bright gaslights of bars and restaurants and hotels threw a glare over Broadway until well toward dawn. The rumble of omnibuses and the clatter of hackney-coaches was never stilled. New York was a city where men made such incredible fortunes that a new word, "millionaire," was on everybody's lips. Two things gave it a quality, a flavor that was unique, and New Yorkers were proud of both. Nowhere else was the tempo of life so fast. And the only permanent characteristic of New York was continuous change. From week to week, almost from day to day, the look of the city was constantly being transformed.[16]

LLOYD MORRIS   *Incredible New York*

You may have noticed in the preceding paragraph, in which details were used, that it was made up primarily of major supporting statements. That paragraph was chosen deliberately. Not all paragraphs have minor supporting statements, because such statements are not always needed. The marshalling of details in major supporting statements may suffice. The effectiveness of a topic sentence supported with details lies largely in the *accumulation* of them. It is a method of support that is direct, orderly, and invariably effective.

¶ Exercises

A. Write five sentences using *detail* as major supporting statements for one of the following topic sentences.

1. Part-time jobs are available during vacations from school.
2. A baby-sitter should know what to do in an emergency.
3. Our town is in a class by itself.

4. A computer can save a lot of work.

5. On my way to school the next morning, I was appalled at the damage done by Hurricane Hazel.

B. Select one of the following topic sentences and develop it into a paragraph using *details*. Use only major supporting statements and underline the controlling idea.

1. In recent years a number of new automobile accessories have been developed for the convenience of motorists.

2. A good fisherman is thorough in his preparations for a day on the stream [or lake or ocean].

3. Few people know the basic facts about stamp collecting [or coin collecting].

4. There are some unusual treasures available to the scuba diver.

5. The later years of the composer Beethoven were not happy ones.

Reason

When you are asked a question that involves your opinion or judgment, you should give it your best thinking. What you have to say will probably be based upon your personal experience, on what you have read, or what you have heard on the subject from people whom you respect. If you write a paragraph in response to such a question, you will very likely develop your topic sentence with reasons.

Your ability to develop sound reasons will depend on your ability to think clearly and logically. In some ways development of a paragraph using good reasons is more difficult than one using details or examples. An explanation for this is that reasons have value; some are better than others. This is not true with facts. For example, a fact is neither good nor bad. If a statement is verifiable, it is a fact. If not, it is not a fact. The same is true of examples. They must have a basis in truth or should not be used.

The development of good reasons is a creative process. The trick is to develop reasons which are sound and, therefore, believable to your reader. A weak reason is like a lame excuse. We have all heard the story about the student who did not have a theme to turn in on the day it was due. "Why not?" asked the teacher. "Well," replied the student, "I spent all last evening writing it, but the dog chewed it up in the night." The point is that weak reasons, like lame excuses, can actually damage your case.

A paragraph using good reasons can serve many purposes. You may be asked, for example, why Longfellow is considered the people's poet, or why traffic congestion in your town has become so serious. You may be asked to justify something you have written, said, or done. You may simply want to write to the editor of your local newspaper to comment on some civic condition. You might be asked why some process in your business isn't working very well. In each case your response must include reasons.

The greatest danger of violating the principle of unity is in the use of reasons. There is a way of testing their validity, however. Just as we recommended the word *specifically* to test details, the words *because* or *therefore* are helpful in testing reasons. If you think the idea of your topic sentence is true because certain matters related to it are true, then the test word *because* will be most helpful. On the other hand, if the truth of the topic sentence implies that certain other things should therefore be true, then the test word, *therefore*, will be most helpful.

Two brief passages follow. The test word *because* was used in the first; the test word *therefore* was used in the second. Both topic sentences are supported by reasons.

A suburban community grows out of the needs of certain city dwellers. Businesspersons seek locations outside the city limits away from the congested downtown traffic and in areas where parking space is readily available. City dwellers, eager to take advantage of adequate parking facilities, attractive and well-stocked department and food stores, as well as drug stores, gift shops, and bakeries essential to every shopper, desert the city establishments for the ones in a suburban area. Finally, lower tax rates, choice of building sites, and modest homes on convenient terms attract prospective clients in search of a place to live.

A suburban community, once established, should develop a sense of obligation to its new residents. In time a committee, composed of leading citizens, should assume a supervisory position for the good of the community. Though unincorporated, the community through its leaders is responsible for cleanup campaigns, initiating action toward the development of a park and construction of a public swimming pool, encouraging new business to come into the community, and making every effort to beautify the whole area.

Notice that the topic sentence in each of the preceding paragraphs has a somewhat different tone. In the first one, the writer might be responding to the question, "Why do you think suburban communities grow?" He or she thinks it is in response to the needs of certain city dwellers and adds, "I think this *because* . . ." and proceeds to supply reasons.

The writer of the second topic sentence is clearly taking a stand on something he or she believes. Believing it, the writer proceeds to say, "Therefore, we should do the following" and supplies reasons.

The following paragraph exemplifies the use of reason as basic material in developing a topic sentence, with its controlling idea. The writer gives reasons for believing that the public's continued ignorance about tranquilizers is a serious problem.

> One very real problem in the tremendous rise in the use of tranquilizers is the public's continued ignorance about the drugs. The Miami research study re-interviewed 200 regular users of Valium and found that less than a third of them knew of the dangers involved. Some of these dangers include the fact that, although not physically addictive, Valium can be psychologically habit-forming. Valium and all tranquilizers can make one dizzy and sleepy—and thus should never be taken before driving or performing any other function that requires total concentration. The most frightening danger, however, is that in combination with alcohol, Valium can be fatal. (It is not known for certain, but doctors believe this very combination, found in her blood tests, may have put Karen Ann Quinlan into the coma that lasted for more than a year and a half.) Researcher Carl Chambers of the Miami group says, "People are dumb about drugs—and their doctors don't tell them the facts." [17]
>
> PENELOPE MCMILLAN   "Women and Tranquilizers"

The writer of the next paragraph gives reasons for the significance of the office of the President of the United States.

> Today's Presidency is of tridimensional importance. It embraces leadership of the people in social and economic reform—an activity that transcends state lines and ignores "State Rights." The President has been the chief propagator of the welfare state and a leading instrument of the transformation of American capitalism into a structure not only of big capital but also big labor. It is to him, of all officials, that reformers and the oppressed have most hopefully looked. But today's Presidency

is more than national leadership. It signalizes the elevation of the Presidential office into a position of international significance. The President is a leader who must get on with many other leaders everywhere. As head of the principal military power of the free world, he provides leadership to a half dozen military alliances around the globe. Through U.S. foreign policies he becomes both the symbol and the instrument of American concern for less fortunate peoples. At the same time, the Presidency connotes a household presence, friendly and familiar. Reciprocal bonds of affection and trust are initiated through the use of nationwide press services, radio, and television, which narrow the distance between the administrative head and the public. It is to the Presidency that Americans instinctively turn in crisis or disaster.[18]

DONNA STANSBY   [A student]

¶ Exercises

A. Supply five sentences using *reason* to create major supporting statements for one of the following topic sentences.

1. The increasing popularity of surburban shopping malls makes weekend parking there difficult.
2. Businesses have finally learned that the consumer is sovereign.
3. In the past twenty years, we have witnessed tremendous technological advances.
4. A universe without limits is comprehensible [or incomprehensible].
5. "Love it or leave it" is not a very bright notion.

B. Select one of the following topics and write a paragraph using *reason*. Use only major supporting statements and underline the controlling idea.

1. The honor system is a good [bad] one for college examinations.
2. Today some understanding of computers is essential to all thinking people.
3. The death penalty is [not] a deterrent to serious crime.
4. There is really nothing wrong with the use of slang.
5. It is essential that the federal government balance the budget—now!

Illustration or Example

In one sense, at least, the paragraph of illustration or example, as we are using the terms in this chapter, may be like the old saying, "One picture is worth a thousand words." Illustration presents material to the reader in the form of action, expressed or implied. The quality of action makes illustration or example particularly different from detail and reason as basic material for building better paragraphs. The reader gets the "feel" of an unfolding or implied story in much the same way that an observer kinesthetically experiences movement and tension as he or she watches cars crash on the highway.

Most of us enjoy illustration. Certainly the success of television is its visual nature. We enjoy books that are illustrated, although a good writer can provide equally vivid illustration using words. Learning to do that is our next step.

A paragraph may have as its basic material one or more illustrations or examples. Whether you employ one or several will depend, to a large extent, on the complexity of the thought expressed in the controlling idea and on your own ingenuity. One long, well-constructed, and vividly rendered illustration may be sufficiently persuasive of your point to support the paragraph by itself. However, the more involved or difficult your central idea is, the more illustrations or examples you may need, each varying slightly in subject matter but tending toward the same objective; namely, effective support of the topic sentence.

A paragraph of illustration or example presents a slightly different problem with regard to the principle of unity. If the illustration is composed of several sentences that make up only one anecdote, you do not test for unity in the paragraph by checking each sentence with the controlling idea, as you do with detail and reason. The illustration as a whole—one single unit—must support the controlling idea. If you use a number of short (or even long) illustrations, then each as a unit goes directly back to the controlling idea of the paragraph. It is the illustration or example *as a unit* that must be in unity with the controlling idea.

The paragraphs that follow use illustration as basic material. In the first, the writer uses an anecdote to provide an insight into the quality of what she has described as the "disordered and incoherent" world of the two-year-old child.

When the child has acquired some language, we get some extraordinary glimpses of this fantastic world: When my friend David was two and a half years old, he was being prepared for a trip to Europe with his parents. He was a very bright child, talked well for his age, and seemed to take in everything his parents had to say with interest and enthusiasm. The whole family would fly to Europe (David knew what an airplane was), they would see many unusual things, they would go swimming, go on trains, and meet some of David's friends there. The preparation story was carried on with just the right amount of emphasis for a couple of weeks before the trip. But after a while David's parents noticed that he stopped asking questions about "Yurp" and even seemed depressed when he heard his parents talk about it. The parents tried to find out what was troubling him. He was most reluctant to talk about it. Then one day, David came out with his secret in an agonizing confession. "I can't go to Yurp!" he said, and the tears came very fast. "I don't know how to fly yet!" [19]

SELMA H. FRAIBERG *The Magic Years*

In the next paragraph, the writer compiles a number of instances supporting her contention that reading is living—a way of adding to one's knowledge and experience. In this paragraph, each sentence supports the main idea.

All good readers know, of course, that they are *living* instead of merely reading. In other words, they know that they are adding untold knowledge and understanding to their lives, becoming wiser, more experienced in the ways of the world. Don Quixote shows them the transforming power of the human imagination—how dreams can make life not only bearable, but exciting, no matter what one pays for such excitement. King Saul proves to them how costly goodness itself can be and alas! often is; for Saul was a good man, even a noble one, who paid dearly and ironically for his very sense of honor. No tragic hero in any Greek play is more truly tragic than Saul. Tess of the D'Urbervilles brings all good readers not only to tears, but to a new understanding of outraged innocence, a new pity for all who live. Dostoyevsky shows them through his three Karamazov brothers how dangerous a mere intellect can be, how much more perilous is the mind than are the affections, no matter how misguidedly one loves. Life may well be circumscribed for many of us, but it is *never* circumscribed for any of us once we learn how to read. [20]

MARY ELLEN CHASE "Why Teach Literature?"

Next, a famous sportswriter dramatizes the playing of baseball by means of an illustration that puts the reader right on the field of action.

> Major-league baseball is one of the most difficult and precise of all games, but you would never know it unless you went down on the field and got close to it and tried it yourself. For instance, the distance between pitcher and catcher is a matter of twenty paces, but it doesn't seem like enough when you have a catcher's mitt and try to hold a pitcher with the speed of Dizzy Dean or Dazzy Vance. Not even the sponge that catchers wear in the palm of the hand when working with fast-ball pitchers and the bulky mitt are sufficient to rob the ball of shock and sting that lames your hand unless you know how to ride with the throw and kill some of its speed. The pitcher standing on his little elevated mound, looms up enormously over you at that short distance, and when he ties himself into a coiled spring preparatory to letting fly, it requires all of your self-control not to break and run for safety. And as for the things they can do with a baseball, those major-league pitchers . . . ! One way of finding out is to wander down on the field an hour or so before game-time when there is no pressure on them, pull on the catcher's glove, and try to hold them. [21]
>
> PAUL GALLICO   "The Feel"

The next paragraph is the introduction to a most incisive comment on the proliferation of bureaucracy. The essay from which it is taken has become a classic in the literature of public administration and organization theory. Humor, as you will see, can be applied even to fields such as these.

> It is a commonplace observation that work expands so as to fill the time available for its completion. Thus, an elderly lady of leisure can spend the entire day in writing and dispatching a postcard to her niece at Bognor Regis. An hour will be spent in finding the postcard, another in hunting for spectacles, half-an-hour in search for the address, an hour and a quarter in composition, and twenty minutes in deciding whether or not to take the umbrella when going to the pillar-box in the next street. The total effort which would occupy a busy man for three minutes all told may in this fashion leave another person prostrate after a day of doubt, anxiety and toil. [22]
>
> C. NORTHCOTE PARKINSON   *Parkinson's Law*

¶ Exercises

A. For one of the following topic sentences, write five *illustrative* units or sentences.

1. The conquest of space, many people tend to forget, is in part the achievement of the ground crew and all the supporting personnel.

2. Life is full of ironies.

3. A person's character is often molded by daily occurrences which, at the moment, seem insignificant.

4. Some animals have ways by which they can communicate.

5. No one's perfect!

B. Select one of the following topic sentences and write a paragraph using *illustrations.* Use no minor supporting statements. Underline the controlling idea.

1. "A stitch in time saves nine."

2. The state lottery often seems to smile on the deserving.

3. The best defense is a good offense.

4. Terrorism, it seems, is increasing in all areas of the world.

5. The best way to succeed in school is to develop effective study habits.

Combination of Basic Materials

Although many topics you will be writing about can be developed by means of details, reasons, or illustrations alone, like the examples presented thus far in this chapter, others will require a combination of these basic materials. In writing about complex subjects, you may find that the clearest presentation calls for a division of the subject into its parts. One or more might be illustration, followed up with an opinion—your own or that of an authority you are citing. You then move to the next part of the main subject and make similar decisions about its treatment. The precise pattern of combining detail, illustration, and reason will depend on the material you have available and your organizational strategy.

Suppose, for example, that you are preparing a report on the American economy in recent years and have developed the following topic sentence:

By 1983 it was clear that the American economy was regaining its health.

In support of this statement you wish to establish the following points:

1. First, the rate of inflation had sharply slowed.
2. Second, the employment rate was sharply up from previous years.
3. Finally, interest rates were much lower than in previous years.

These three main points are the component parts of the statement made in the topic sentence. At this point it may occur to you that all three could be supported quite simply by details; that is, you easily make your point with facts and figures. But it may also occur to you that there is a relationship between these parts. From them conclusions may be drawn.

In the first part, you may decide that the proof that lies in details is simply not needed because the fact that the inflation rate was down in 1983 is well known. Examples might prove more appropriate and you begin to experiment:

Then, for the first time in many years, some of those on fixed incomes began to breathe a little easier. The wage earner, who had seen his or her annual 8 percent raise fall to a loss in the face of double-digit inflation, suddenly realized that a raise was a raise. The grocery shopper was aware that the leak in the bottom of the shopping cart had finally been plugged.

At this point you conclude, At last the long and sleepless night of inflation was coming to an end.

The second part of your point, you will recall, was that the employment rate was up. Here, you decide, examples are not very useful, but details are. You write:

The good news was that more people were not only back working but paying taxes on their earnings and enjoying a standard of living that having a job ordinarily implied. The still bad news was that the employment outlook for some classes of Americans had not improved but had even deteriorated. The situation was particularly acute for young blacks and Hispanics.

The third part of your point, the fact that interest rates were down, might be best supported, you decide, with reasons. Why were interest rates down? What has come before might be helpful. You continue by concluding:

> With inflation and unemployment under partial control it was inevitable that interest rates should fall. It is difficult to know which came first, but with lower interest rates, people could now afford to buy homes, automobiles, and other purchases on credit which, in turn, created a demand that had to be satisfied by more people working to supply them. Work meant money and money meant demand. With more money circulating, more was available for credit. And that made for lower interest rates.

Now let us put the parts together as one paragraph. The topic sentence is identified as TS, major supporting statements by roman numerals (I, II, etc.) and minor statements by upper case letters (A, B, etc.).

> (TS) By 1983 it was clear that the American economy was regaining its health. (I) First, the rate of inflation had sharply slowed. (A) Then, for the first time in many years, those on fixed incomes began to breathe a little easier. (B) The wage earner who had seen his or her annual 8 percent raise fall to a loss in the face of double-digit inflation suddenly realized that any raise was welcome. (C) The grocery shopper was aware that the leak in the bottom of the shopping cart had finally been plugged. (II) Second, the rate of employment for some was sharply up from previous years and was welcome. (A) The good news was that more people were not only back working but paying taxes on their earnings and enjoying a standard of living that having a job ordinarily implied. (B) The bad news was that the employment outlook for some classes of Americans had not improved but had even deteriorated. (C) The situation was particularly acute for young blacks and Hispanics. (III) Finally, interest rates were much lower than in previous years. (A) For most, with inflation and unemployment under partial control, it was inevitable that interest rates should fall. (B) With lower interest rates, people could now afford to buy homes, automobiles, and other purchases on credit.

(C) Work meant money and money meant demand. (D) With more money circulating, more was available for credit at lower interest rates. (E) Indeed, the economy for most was healthier.

At this point you should notice two things. With a well-constructed paragraph such as this you can go back, add more material if necessary, and tidy up any weaknesses in coherence, word choice, grammatical matters, and so on. Also, if you think the paragraph is too long, you can divide it into three parts, each part capable of standing separately because it would have its own topic sentence. (Essentially, what you have is a well-organized, fully treated *long* paragraph, or a well-organized, highlighted *short theme.*)

Now let us examine a number of paragraphs that are built up by means of basic materials in a variety of combinations. In the first a composer discusses how people listen to music. Following his topic sentence with its definite controlling idea, he expresses his opinion as to how he can best approach the discussion. This statement is followed by another opinion; namely, how he believes all people listen to music. He then breaks down the listening process into three component parts, or details. He concludes his paragraph with his reason for identifying the "planes" of listening as he does.

> We all listen to music according to our separate capacities. But, for the sake of analysis, the whole listening process may become clearer if we break it up into its component parts, so to speak. In a certain sense we all listen to music on three separate planes. For lack of a better terminology, one might name these: (1) the sensuous plane, (2) the expressive plane, (3) the sheerly musical plane. The only advantage to be gained from mechanically splitting up the listening process into these hypothetical planes is the clearer view to be had of the way in which we listen. [23]

> AARON COPLAND   *What to Listen for in Music*

The next paragraph is an editorial (a long paragraph) in which the writer uses details, illustrations, and reasons, in that order, in each of two sections that make up the whole paragraph. The topic sentence cites two features of the action of the Kennedy Administration in announcing the quarantine of Cuba. Each section is taken up separately, illustrated, and followed by an editorial comment. Each sentence is numbered to facilitate discussion.

[1]The Kennedy Administration's performance in proclaiming a "quarantine" on "offensive" weapons shipped to Cuba had both its disquieting and its reassuring features, quite apart from immediate political implications. [2]At the disquieting end it heightened the psychological tension almost to the breaking point. [3]For forty-eight hours prior to the Government's announcement of a "quarantine for Cuba," Presidential Press Secretary Pierre Salinger carried on a publicity buildup through the machinery of his office. [4]He had Congressional leaders called to Washington; he maneuvered newsmen around like pawns; he even marched and countermarched bureaucratic bigwigs with the Top Secret briefcases front and center on the Washington stage. [5]Then having marshalled these powers within the nation's capital, the press secretary apparently had no immediate comment on what everyone suspected was a national crisis. [6]The result was a Gargantuan case of jitters for all concerned; and for the already volatile stock market, the great silence probably sent securities plunging downward past the Dow-Jones 571-plus "support level." [7]On the reassuring end of things, however, was Mr. Kennedy himself. [8]The President went before a national hook-up of radio and television and enunciated the new Administration policy. [9]He outlined Russia's surreptitious steps in installing "offensive" armament, namely, intercontinental ballistic missiles, in Cuba. [10]He supported his claims by means of intelligence reports that had been gathered on Castro's island and sent during the previous week to the President's office. [11]What he said helped dispel some of the gloom and failure surrounding U.S. foreign policy. [12]What he said makes it clear to Premier Khrushchev that he can go no further. [13]And, finally, what he said will give Americans a sense of resolution, of an attitude defined, of lines laid down.[24]

MAYNARD KNISKERN Editorial, Springfield (Ohio) *Sun*

Now, if you look back over the preceding paragraph, you will see that sentence 1 is the topic sentence with a compound controlling idea ("disquieting" and "reassuring" features). Sentence 2 announces that the first part of the controlling idea is to be discussed: the "disquieting" feature. Sentences 3 and 4 cite as illustrations the actions of the press secretary that contributed to the "disquieting" feature of the whole affair. Sentences 5 and 6 are the writer's editorial comment, his opinion, on the press secretary's actions in this crisis and on the reaction of Wall Street to the "silence" in Washington. Sentence 7 announces that the second part of the controlling idea is to be considered (the "reassuring" feature). Sentences 8, 9, and 10 cite as illustrations the president's action in the government's performance. Sentences 11, 12, and 13 are again the comments of the writer, evaluating the effects of the president's words.

The structure of the paragraph on the quarantine of Cuba can very conveniently be symbolized by the letters D—I—R, that is D *(detail)*, I *(illustration)*, R *(reason)*. This type of paragraph is often called for by the nature of the subject being discussed, but students will all too frequently fail to provide the necessary development, not because they do not have adequate material, but simply because they do not know how. The formula D—I—R can be a helpful guide.

If you can give your writing a touch of humor, you may be able to turn a staid bit of information into an entertaining piece. Perhaps from experience or correspondence the writer of the next paragraph adapted some material into a topic sentence that set up a situation, and then he illustrated the problem. In his last two sentences he gives two opinions related to the experiment: that of the wife who approved, and that of the dairyman, whose wife's pleasure and the cost of the remedy merely added to his difficulty.

> A Sullivan County gentleman who engages extensively in dairying ran into difficulties when his cows developed a skin ailment that made them well-nigh impossible to milk. To no avail, he tried various remedies prescribed by his veterinarian, and then, in a moment of exasperation, seized a dollar-seventy-five bottle of his wife's Elizabeth Arden hand lotion and rubbed the liquid on the bovine's affected parts. A relieved moo and a splendid flow of milk ensued. He has since stocked up with a supply of the lotion sufficient to soothe the entire herd. His wife, who has written us of this interesting therapeutic adventure, observes, "It has been rather sweet to go into the cow barn, smell its perfumed air, and see the long shelf of pink bottles." She says her husband is expressing indignation, though, because he has to pay a twenty-per-cent tax on the remedy. [25]
>
> "Home Remedy"   *The New Yorker*

Finally, E. B. White expresses surprise that a big city like New York works at all. His controlling idea states it as a "miracle." He reasons that, despite the fact New York *does* work, it is "implausible." Sentences 3 and 4 illustrate the fact that it does work, sentence 5 states another reason why it should not work (although it does), sentence 6 illustrates 5, sentences 7 through 12 are further reasons why the city should not work (but does), and sentence 13 is a concluding opinion. All this may sound confusing, but it really is not.

You should note that some sentences like number 5, though expressed as a reason, have within them a number of specific details that could have been presented as minor supports if the writer had chosen to do so. For example, in sentence 5, the writer's reason at this point could have read; "The subterranean system is most complicated"; he could then have written several sentences of detail to support that general major statement: one sentence about the snarl of telephone cables, another about the miles of power lines, perhaps a few more on steam pipes, gas mains, sewer pipes. Instead, he chose to condense them all into one unit, combining major and minor supports. What results, then, may be a sentence of reason fortified by details. Here is his paragraph:

[1]It is a miracle that New York works at all. [2]The whole thing is implausible. [3]Every time the residents brush their teeth, millions of gallons of water must be drawn from the Catskills and the hills of Westchester. [4]When a young man in Manhattan writes a letter to his girl in Brooklyn, the love message gets blown to her through a pneumatic tube—*pfft*—just like that. [5]The subterranean system of telephone cables, power lines, steam pipes, gas mains, and sewer pipes is reason enough to abandon the island to the gods and weevils. [6]Every time an incision is made in the pavement, the noisy surgeons expose ganglia that are tangled beyond belief. [7]By rights New York should have destroyed itself long ago, from panic or fire or rioting or failure of some vital supply line in its circulatory system or from some labyrinthine short circuit. [8]Long ago the city should have experienced an insoluble traffic snarl at some impossible bottleneck. [9]It should have perished of hunger when food lines failed for a few days. [10]It should have been wiped out by a plague starting in its slums or carried in by ships' rats. [11]It should have been overwhelmed by the sea that licks at it on every side. [12]The workers in its myriad cells should have succumbed to nerves, from the fearful pall of smoke-fog that drifts over every few days from Jersey, blotting out all light at noon and leaving the high offices suspended, men groping and depressed, and the sense of world's end. [13]It should have been touched in the head by the August heat and gone off its rocker. [26]

E. B. WHITE   *Here Is New York*

Summary

The well-written paragraph makes use of details, reasons, and illustrations—singly or in combination—to support as effectively as possible the controlling idea of the topic sentence. A paragraph using *detail* gives as its major supporting statements the factual parts of the idea being developed. For example, a paragraph of detail about an apple would tell the parts that comprise the apple—the stem, skin, flesh, core, seeds, and others. These parts, when all are put together, equal the whole apple.

A paragraph using *reason* states reasons or opinions as opposed to factual details to develop the controlling idea expressed in the topic sentence. These reasons, good or poor, are the writer's thoughts about the subject or the thoughts of someone else. If you believe it is healthful to eat an apple a day, you give your reasons, or your doctor's—an apple a day keeps the doctor away—to prove your point. The reasons will be the major supporting statements of your controlling idea.

A paragraph using *illustration* or *example* gives one long anecdote or several short ones. If the illustration is a single long one, all the sentences work together as a unit to prove the validity of the controlling idea; if you use a number of short illustrations, each one individually supports the controlling idea directly. For instance, you might tell a story of how an apple you gave to someone started a friendship. On the other hand, you might find several illustrations of how an apple influenced the lives of people at different times in history.

Finally, in the same paragraph you might use all the basic materials—detail, reason, and illustration—in an appropriate pattern of development. If so, the details or the reasons will probably serve as the major supporting statements of the controlling idea and the illustrations will be used as minor supports. However, in paragraphs using a combination of materials, you will follow no prescribed order; instead, you should seek the best combination of materials to provide the reader with the most effective defense of your topic sentence with its controlling idea. Remember, the well-written paragraph, like a poem or short story, takes time and great care.

¶ Exercises

A. For each of the following paragraphs copy the topic sentence (the first sentence) with its identifying number. Underline the controlling idea. Then list consecutively the numbers of the sentences. After each number identify the kind of basic material used in that sentence. (If several sentence numbers belong together because they identify several sentences in one long illustration, merely bracket those numbers.)

1. While many black women in business today are where they are because they struck out on their own and built a viable company from scratch, some inherited companies from their husbands. [1]In 1948, Leon H. Washington, publisher of the Los Angeles *Sentinel,* had a stroke which left him unable to carry on the day-to-day work of running a newspaper. [2]His wife, Ruth, a studio photographer, decided that she would take over even though she didn't know anything about the news business. [3]"I surrounded myself with good professionals," she says, "top journalists and other top people." [4]As Ruth Washington learned more and more about running a newspaper, she began making changes in the paper's format, advertising, and editorial policies. [5]Today the weekly *Sentinel* is one of the leaders among black newspapers in real estate and classified ads. [6]The size of the newspaper has more than doubled. [7]The staff of six employed when Mrs. Washington took over 27 years ago has grown to 40. [8]And she's not about to quit—no retirement for her anytime soon. [9]"I have ink in my blood," explains the 61-year-old publisher. [27]

CAROL A. NORTON "Black Women in Corporate America"

2. The children in our village do not play [Run, Sheep, Run]. [1]I am not sure of the reason. [2]It must be because children no longer possess the streets, as they no longer own the vacant lots and the gardens. [3]Traffic is too great a hazard, even in our quiet sector, for such wild excursions. [4]Perhaps there are no coverts left in which to hide. [5]Or could it be the curse of full employment among the young? [6]Children belong to the country clubs, and swim away the afternoons. [7]They go to camps. [8]They practice tennis and take riding lessons and are netted into hobby groups. [9]Even those we call the underprivileged go to organized playgrounds, presided over by adults. [10]One must have leisure for Run, Sheep, Run—leisure and long lazy summers. [11]Life must not be hurried, as it is today for everyone. [12]There must be time for the gathering of the clan, time for the chase, and time to come home, shouting, through a dim blue twilight that smells of fresh-cut grass. [28]

PHYLLIS MCGINLEY   *The Province of the Heart*

3. After Waterloo Napoleon was to live for six years and achieve an ironic final victory. [1]He fled to the west coast of France where at Rochefort he surrendered to the British navy, blockading the harbor. [2]Exiled to the island of St. Helena, he managed to transform his image from that of a fallen tyrant into a martyr. [3]Out of St. Helena grew the Napoleonic legend that exists today. [4]One can see it in the red porphyry sarcophagus at the Invalides in Paris where his body was buried in 1840. [5]There are listed the names of his great battles: Rivoli. Pyramides, Marengo, Austerlitz, Iéna, Friedland, Wagram, Moscova. [6]But nowhere in that temple of legend and glory is written the word Waterloo. [(29)]

THOMAS N. CARMICHAEL   "Waterloo: 1815"

4. Even more important than cheating, perhaps, is the frame of mind that leads to it. [1]There coexists, side by side with our higher educational system, an actively propagated faith which may be termed "antieducation." [2]Recently in a Boston restaurant I overheard a conversation in which the main tenets of the creed were set forth. [3]A high-school graduate about to set out for college was receiving advice from an upperclassman.

[4]"Now when you get there, remember," the older boy was saying, "books are for the birds, not for the people. [5]What matters is contacts. [6]Get there a couple, three days early, introduce yourself around, become known, get elected to a class office. [7]Plan your courses so you're not always on the books, so you have time to make contacts."

[8]The younger lad protested that he wanted to be an engineer, a course which called for quite a bit of study along a prescribed curriculum.

[9]"Now, Charley, it's your life, but you ought to get engineering out of your head," the upperclassman said. [10]"It's a grind all four years, morning to night, you're never finished. [11]When you're out of college, does anybody care how many books you read? [12]Make your contacts. [13]Then, man, you got a deal that matters, and if you haven't got that, you got nothing." [(30)]

JEROME ELLISON   "American Disgrace: Cheating"

B.   Select one of the following topic sentences and write a paragraph using detail, reason, *and* illustration or example in some appropriate combination to develop the controlling idea. Underline the controlling idea. As you introduce minor supporting material, be sure that it is in unity with the major support and with the controlling idea of the paragraph. In the margin opposite each sentence, identify the type of basic material you are using.

1. The United States should [need not] avoid meddling in the affairs of other nations.

2. A property owner should [should not] have the right to use any means to protect it.

3. Television has contributed to the decline of conversation.

4. The time has come for colleges and universities to clean up their act in athletics.

5. With proper maintenance, an automobile today should perform satisfactorily for 150,000 miles.

3. Sentence Unity

A paragraph typically consists of a number of sentences, each of which expresses or supports the main idea of the paragraph. In Chapter 1 we considered the importance of unity in paragraphs, that is, using only statements which support the *controlling idea.* Any that did not do so had to be eliminated. In this chapter, we will be looking at *sentences* and at ways of achieving unity within *them.*

Unity is ordinarily not a problem in simple sentences consisting of a single subject and verb; it may become a serious problem, however, in sentences of a compound or complex nature. You have probably already studied the four ways that a sentence may be structured, but this is a good time to review them. The four types of sentences are:

- Simple
- Compound
- Complex
- Compound-complex

A *simple* sentence has either one subject, one verb, or both. Let's see how this works by examining these sentences:

Tom made three touchdowns (one subject, *Tom;* one verb, *made*).

Tom made three touchdowns and kicked two extra points (one subject, *Tom;* two verbs, *made* and *kicked*).

54

Tom and Kevin each made a touchdown (two subjects, *Tom* and *Kevin;* one verb, *made*).

These sentences have in common one subject *or* one verb.

A *compound* sentence has two or more independent or main clauses. You will recall that a clause is a group of words that has at least a subject and a verb. An independent clause is one that may be combined with other clauses but that could stand alone as a simple sentence. A dependent or subordinate clause must have a subject and verb but cannot stand alone. The difference between them will soon be clear to you. Consider these compound sentences in which the independent clauses are bracketed.

- [Marcie had eighteen points,] and [Pam had nine rebounds.]
- [The war was over,] but [the job of reconstruction remained.]

Clearly, each of the bracketed clauses could stand alone although they are short.

A *complex* sentence contains an independent and a dependent clause. To illustrate, let us look at the compound sentence examples written as complex sentences (again the clauses are bracketed).

- [Although Pam had nine rebounds,] [Marcie had eighteen points.]
- [When the war was over,] [the job of reconstruction remained.]

It is obvious that the subordinate clauses, "Although Pam had nine re- bounds" and "When the war was over," simply don't make any sense without their independent clauses.

A *compound-complex* sentence is essentially one that has at least one de- pendent clause and two independent clauses. Here is an example with each clause bracketed:

- [While Rodney was rich and famous,] [he was not happy;] and [his friends were sorry for him.]

To be unified, a sentence should satisfy two requirements. First, if we exclude fragments written for stylistic effect, the sentence must be grammati- cally complete—that is, contain a subject and a verb. (Remember that a phrase or a dependent clause by itself is not a sentence.) Second, and equally important, a unified sentence should have its most important idea in the independent clause, and its less important idea in the dependent clause or other modifying construction.

How do you decide which idea is more important and belongs in the independent clause? In any one isolated sentence, the more important idea is simply the one you wish to emphasize. The sentences we are considering here, however, do not appear in isolation but in the context of a paragraph; and in a paragraph, the controlling idea governs. This means that when two ideas are expressed in the same sentence, the one that more directly supports the controlling idea is more important and should be emphasized.

An example of how this works might help. Recall our two sample sentences above, which, as samples, were presented apart from any context.

- Marcie scored eighteen points, and Pam had nine rebounds.
- Although Pam had nine rebounds, Marcie scored eighteen points.

The first is *compound;* the second is *complex.* The first would be good support for the topic sentence, "Both Marcie and Pam played an outstanding game against Grover High." However, it is clear that the second sentence would not be good support since it plays down Pam's accomplishment to that of Marcie. But it might be good support for this topic sentence: "With good support from her teammates, Marcie played an outstanding game against Grover High."

Coordination and Subordination

The part of a sentence in which an idea is placed indicates its relative importance. Main ideas belong in independent clauses; minor ideas belong in dependent clauses or in other modifying constructions. Ideas of equal importance belong in the same kind of grammatical constructions. The relation of minor ideas to main ideas is *subordination* as is also the relation of dependent clauses to independent clauses (or modifying constructions to the expressions modified). The relation of ideas equal in importance is *coordination,* as is also the relation of independent clauses to other independent clauses. The use of grammatical relations to guide the reader in recognizing idea-relations helps the writer to unify a sentence, to keep it from coming apart in the reader's mind.

You may have been asked in previous English classes to identify the main idea in sentences. Let us look at several and see how this is done.

- As I came around the barn, a bear loomed before me.
- Ed raced for the bus, and his wife called after him.
- The boy stood up, his eyes stared in fright, and people paused to watch him.

Just how are you to decide which clause-idea in each of the sentences is the really important one? As noted, it is difficult to do without the guidance provided by a controlling idea; that is, if the sentence is isolated.

In the sentence about the bear, the tendency is to say that "The bear appeared before me" is the main idea because it is the independent clause. But if the sentence were to read "When the bear loomed before me, I was coming around the barn"—which is just as good a sentence, *as a sentence*—then "I was coming around the barn" is the main idea. Apparently a conflict exists as to the value of the ideas. To resolve the problem, simply determine what the controlling idea of the topic sentence is and then choose as the main idea the one that directly supports it. In a sense, this is putting the cart before the horse, because in practice you start writing a paragraph with the formulation of your controlling idea. Thus if you are trying to show what loomed before you when you came around the barn, "the bear loomed before me" is the main idea; but, if you are trying to show where you were when the bear appeared, then "I was coming around the barn" is the main idea.

In the sentence about Ed and his wife, both ideas are in independent clauses ("Ed raced for the bus, and his wife called after him"). The writer's problem is whether the clauses should be left that way. If the sentence is to be used in a paragraph that explains what Ed did regardless of the actions of the wife, then "Ed raced for the bus" is the more important idea. On the other hand, if the purpose of the paragraph is to stress the wife's action rather than that of Ed, then "his wife called after him" is the more important idea. On this basis, the sentence could be written in two ways:

- Even though his wife called after him, Ed raced for the bus.
- As Ed raced for the bus, his wife called after him.

Which of these sentences should be used in a given paragraph will depend on the right relation between the idea in the main clause and the controlling idea of the paragraph.

In the sentence about the boy, any one of the three ideas could be the main idea.

- As the boy stood up and his eyes stared in fright, *people paused to watch him.*
- With eyes staring in fright, the *boy stood up* as people paused to watch him.
- As the boy stood up and people paused to watch him, his *eyes stared in fright.*

Each sentence is acceptable as a sentence, but each one stresses a different idea. Again, the main idea will be the one that has a direct relation to the controlling idea of the paragraph in which the sentence is used. Therefore, proper coordination and proper subordination are two ways of showing the proper value of ideas in your sentences. The two chief grammatical constructions for this purpose are the independent clause and the dependent clause.

Unifying Sentences to Fit a Controlling Idea

Let us now use a topic sentence with a definite controlling idea to determine which of a set of ideas belongs in independent clauses and which in dependent ones. The topic sentence we will be developing appears below with the controlling idea italicized. Directly following the topic sentence you will find a numbered series of ideas, all stated as simple sentences. Our task is to combine these short sentences into unified longer ones.

TOPIC SENTENCE: **Throughout his life Edgar Allan Poe faced a *series of disappointments.***

IDEAS

1. His first volume of poems was published in 1827.
2. Very few people bought copies.
3. He successfully gained admission to West Point in the summer of 1830.
4. He was expelled from the Academy the following spring.
5. He became a successful magazine editor in Richmond, Virginia.
6. The owner of the magazine in time objected to his habits.

7. The owner fired him in 1837.

8. Later in New York he wrote his famous poem, "The Raven."

9. It brought him much publicity.

10. It failed to bring him much money.

11. For years he struggled to become proprietor of a magazine.

12. He hoped the magazine would make him rich.

13. He finally became owner of the *Broadway Journal.*

14. It went bankrupt in three months.

Fixing the controlling idea (series of disappointments) clearly in mind, notice that each of the numbered ideas is about either encouraging or disappointing events in the life of Poe. This, of course, makes coordination and subordination easier to achieve. Let us examine the first two:

1. His first volume of poems was published in 1827.

2. Very few people bought copies.

There are several ways in which these ideas can be combined into a satisfactory sentence. What we want is the best one for our paragraph. One possibility is to make the two sentences into independent clauses joined by *but.*

- His first volume of poetry was published in 1827, but very few people bought it.

As an isolated sentence, this one is acceptable and might very well support a topic sentence other than the one we are working with here. But notice that it gives equal emphasis to ideas 1 and 2, whereas only idea 2 supports the controlling idea. Reason tells us, then, that idea 2 should be expressed as an independent clause and idea 1 should be subordinated to it as a dependent clause. We could, therefore, write the sentence in several ways. One way we *wouldn't* do it is this:

- His first volume of poems was published in 1827, although very few people bought copies.

But to be consistent with the controlling idea, we must play down idea 1 and play up idea 2:

- When his first volume of poems was published in 1827, very few people bought copies.

At this point, it will be useful to you to know about some of the types of words and the words themselves that are used in achieving coordination and subordination. First are the coordinating conjunctions. They are used to join independent clauses or other constructions of equal rank. They are *and, but, yet, or, nor,* and *for.* They may therefore be used to join words, phrases, and independent and dependent clauses of equal rank.

Although and *when,* which we have already used, are subordinating conjunctions. They have the effect of turning the words they introduce into dependent clauses that function as *adverbs* in the larger sentences. Some other common subordinating conjunctions are *if, unless, since, because, before, until, while,* and *though.*

Another type of word, the *relative pronoun,* is used to introduce dependent clauses used as *adjectives.* The relative pronouns are *who, whose, whom, which, what,* and *that.*

Returning to the list of ideas about Poe, we find that ideas 3 and 4 have a relationship to each other similar to that of 1 and 2: the first expresses a positive achievement (gaining admission to West Point), the second the disappointing outcome (expulsion the following spring). Since the controlling idea involves *disappointments,* we should subordinate idea 3 and put idea 4 in the independent clause, thus:

- After successfully gaining admission to West Point in the summer of 1830, he was expelled from the Academy the following spring.

The next group of associated ideas consists of ideas 5, 6, and 7. Idea 5 is the kind of positive achievement we have been playing down because of the controlling idea. Therefore, we will want to subordinate it as we did the others. But ideas 6 and 7 are closely related and support the controlling idea. Since the owner has both *objected* and *fired,* these two coordinate ideas can be expressed as part of a compound predicate in the independent clause.

- The owner of the magazine in time objected to his habits and fired him in 1837.

We could introduce idea 5 with a subordinating conjunction such as *although* or *even though.* Having already used *although,* we can, for the sake of variety, subordinate idea 5 by putting it into a dependent clause introduced by the subordinate conjunction *even though:*

> • Even though he became a successful magazine editor in Richmond, Virginia . . .

The dependent clause can then be added to the independent clause like this:

> • Even though he became a successful magazine editor in Richmond, Virginia, the owner of the magazine in time objected to his habits and fired him in 1837.

Ideas 8, 9, and 10 make up the next group:

> 8. Later in New York he wrote his famous poem, "The Raven."
> 9. It brought him much publicity.
> 10. It failed to bring him much money.

In keeping with the controlling idea, *disappointments,* we will want to put idea 10 in the independent clause. With a little rewording, we can combine 8 and 10 into an independent clause:

> • Later in New York, his famous poem, "The Raven," failed to bring him much money.

And into this independent clause we can insert idea 9 as a dependent clause:

> • Later in New York, his famous poem, "The Raven," *which brought him much publicity,* failed to bring him much money.

We now come to the last four ideas, which are closely related:

> 11. For years he struggled to become proprietor of a magazine.
> 12. He hoped the magazine would make him rich.

13. Finally he became owner of the *Broadway Journal.*

14. It went bankrupt in three months.

The main idea is 14. But how should we subordinate 11, 12, and 13? First of all, we notice that idea 12 combines easily with 11:

- For years he struggled to become proprietor of a magazine that he hoped would make him rich.

(On reflection we can eliminate *he hoped* as unnecessary.) Next, it occurs to us that the idea of struggling to be proprietor of a magazine and actually becoming owner of one are closely related—the second being the outcome of the first. The two ideas can be combined as follows:

- When he became proprietor of the *Broadway Journal,* after years of struggle to own a magazine that would make him rich, . . .

When we put all of the combined units together, the paragraph reads as follows:

> Throughout his life Edgar Allan Poe faced a series of disappointments. When his first volume of poems was published in 1827, very few people bought copies. After successfully gaining admission to West Point in the summer of 1830, he was expelled from the Academy the following spring. Even though he became a successful magazine editor in Richmond, Virginia, the owner of the magazine in time objected to his habits and fired him in 1837. Later in New York his famous poem, "The Raven," which brought him much publicity, failed to bring him much money. When he became proprietor of the *Broadway Journal,* after years of struggle to own a magazine that would make him rich, it went bankrupt in three months.

Here, then, is a unified paragraph. It has a definite topic sentence with a specific controlling idea. It has a series of main statements that directly support the controlling idea. It has a number of subordinate ideas that directly support the main statements. Main ideas are in the independent clauses; subordinate ideas are in dependent clauses or in other modifying constructions. The paragraph is unified and shows proper coordination and proper subordination.

Recognizing and Correcting Errors in Coordination and Subordination

The principles we have just been using can also be applied in analyzing a paragraph and composing a revision based on the analysis. For demonstration we will use the following student paragraph in which each sentence, clause, or other subordinating element has been numbered:

> A trip through England and France is an exciting adventure. ¹The flight across the ocean takes only a few hours. ²In England one can travel through the ancient realm of King Arthur and his knights, ³as well as through the countryside of Chaucer's Canterbury pilgrims. ⁴The pilgrims lived in the fourteenth century. ⁵France is across the channel from England. ⁶In Paris one can see the site of the old Bastille, ⁷which is near the Seine River, ⁸thus recalling the days of Robespierre, Madame Defarge, and Sydney Carton. ⁹Little Parisian streets lure the adventurer into the strangest places. ¹⁰One is a very narrow street and climbs a high hill ¹¹on which is Montmartre. ¹²Another street goes to several cafes, ¹³such as the famous Le Coq and the Bon Vivant. ¹⁴Paris has some little streets ¹⁵ending at world-famous theaters and restaurants.

Remember, you are checking *ideas,* not grammatical units. Also remember that if you are in doubt about an idea—no matter what its grammatical form may be—use the *because* test. When you are seeking adventure, "the pilgrims lived in the fourteenth century" is in itself no proof of "exciting adventure," but "traveling through the ancient realm of King Arthur and his knights" is. Make this distinction clear in your mind before you start this analysis.

As a first step, we will go through the paragraph listing each idea separately and assigning a number to it. This list will correspond to the numbered list of ideas for the Poe paragraph on pages 58–59, except that we are entering ideas in whatever form they appear in the paragraph, not always in simple sentences as we did earlier. The topic sentence and numbered list follow:

TOPIC SENTENCE: A trip through England and France is an *exciting adventure.*

IDEAS

1. The flight across the ocean takes only a few hours.
2. In England one can travel through the ancient realm of King Arthur and his knights,

3. as well as through the countryside of Chaucer's Canterbury pilgrims.
4. The pilgrims lived in the fourteenth century.
5. France is across the channel from England.
6. In Paris one can visit the site of the old Bastille,
7. which is near the Seine River,
8. thus recalling the days of Robespierre, Madame Defarge, and Sydney Carton.
9. Little Parisian streets lure the adventurer into the strangest places.
10. One is a very narrow street and climbs a high hill
11. on which is Montmartre.
12. Another street goes to several cafes,
13. such as the famous Le Coq and Bon Vivant.
14. Paris has some little streets
15. ending at world-famous theaters and restaurants.

Our next step will be to classify each idea as either *main* or *subordinate*. Again, no matter what their grammatical form may be, subordinate ideas resemble the minor supports we discussed on pages 14–16. The main ideas are those that directly explain the controlling idea when the *because* test is applied. The subordinate ideas are those that directly support some word or clause in the paragraph and indirectly support the controlling idea. We should not be surprised to find that some of the ideas we list under main ideas are expressed in dependent clauses, and that some subordinate ideas are expressed in independent clauses. The chief purpose of our chart on the following page is to reveal such situations so that we can deal with them in the revision.

As we enter the numbered ideas in their proper columns, we will notice that some are related to each other. To keep each group of related ideas separate from the rest, we will draw a line above and below them.

A glance at our chart reveals that, as we expected, there are mistakes in coordination and subordination. For our purposes in this analysis, coordination requires that all ideas of similar value should be placed in similar grammatical constructions; more specifically, all main ideas should be expressed in independent clauses. Subordination means that supporting, or less important, material should be placed in dependent clauses, or some other subordinate construction like prepositional phrases, verbal phrases, single adjectives, or single adverbs. Thus, "faulty coordination" means that subordinate mate-

MAIN IDEAS	SUBORDINATE IDEAS
	1. The flight across the ocean takes only a few hours.
2. In England one can travel through the ancient realm of King Arthur and his knights.	
3. as well as through the countryside of Chaucer's Canterbury pilgrims.	
	4. The pilgrims lived in the fourteenth century.
	5. France is across the channel from England.
6. In Paris one can visit the site of the old Bastille,	
	7. which is near the Seine River,
8. thus recalling the days of Robespierre, Madame Defarge, and Sydney Carton.	
9. Little Parisian streets lure the adventurer into the strangest places.	
	10. One is a very narrow street and climbs a high hill
11. on which is Montmartre.	
	12. Another street goes to several cafes
13. such as the famous Le Coq and Bon Vivant.	
	14. Paris has some little streets
15. ending at world-famous theaters and restaurants.	

rial has been put in independent clauses—certain ideas have been presented as coordinate or equal when it is apparent that they are not equal; and "faulty subordination" means that main ideas have been placed in subordinate constructions.

To correct these errors, we must try to put the main ideas in independent clauses and the subordinate ideas in dependent clauses or in some other subordinate construction. As we work with each group of thoughts, we must always keep clearly in mind the controlling idea—*exciting adventure.*

The first group includes ideas 1, 2, 3, and 4. Since 2 and 3 are main ideas (ideas that directly support the controlling idea), we want them expressed in an independent clause. Idea 2 is already stated in an independent clause, but 3 is subordinated by the conjunction *as well as.* We can easily combine them into an independent clause with a compound prepositional phrase:

- **In England one can travel through the ancient realm of King Arthur and his knights and through the countryside of Chaucer's Canterbury pilgrims.**

Ideas 1 and 4 are subordinate and should be tucked into the independent clause where they fit best. A slight rewording makes idea 1 into a good introductory phrase:

- **After a few hours' flight across the ocean . . .**

And idea 4 is easily changed to a dependent clause modifying pilgrims. The revised sentence reads as follows:

- **After a few hours' flight across the ocean, in England one can travel through the ancient realm of King Arthur and his knights and through the countryside of Chaucer's Canterbury pilgrims, who lived in the fourteenth century.**

The second group includes ideas 5, 6, 7, and 8. Ideas 6 and 8 are the main ones. Of course, 6 is already an independent clause; with a little rewording, we can add 8 to it as a part of a compound predicate:

- **In Paris one can visit the site of the old Bastille and recall the days of Robespierre, Madame Defarge, and Sydney Carton.**

That leaves the subordinate ideas to be dealt with. Idea 5 can be reduced to a prepositional phrase,

- **Across the channel . . .**

Idea 7 obviously modifies *Bastille:*

- ... the old Bastille, which is near the Seine River, ...

The revised sentence now reads:

- Across the English Channel in Paris one can visit the site of the old Bastille, which is near the Seine River, and recall the days of Robespierre, Madame Defarge, and Sydney Carton.

The ideas numbered 9 through 15 make up the third group. The subordinate ideas in this group are closely related to the main ideas and can easily be combined with them. Idea 9 sounds all right as it stands. Ideas 10 and 11 can be combined into a single, simple sentence that suggests adventure:

- One very narrow street climbs a high hill to Montmartre.

Ideas 12 and 13 can be combined in a similar way:

- Another street goes to the famous Le Coq and Bon Vivant cafes.

We now have a series of sentences, related in meaning and parallel in structure.

9. ... Parisian streets lure ...
10./11. ... narrow street climbs ...
12./13. Another street goes ...

This pattern suggests the solution to the combination of ideas 14 and 15. By making *Some little Paris streets* the subject and changing the participle *ending* to a verb, we get this satisfying result:

- Some little Paris streets end at world-famous theaters and restaurants.

With all of the ideas in the third group combined in this way, the resulting sentences read like this:

- Little Parisian streets lure the adventurer into the strangest places. One very narrow street climbs a high hill to Montmartre. Another street goes to the famous Le Coq and Bon Vivant cafes. Some little Paris streets end at world-famous theaters and restaurants.

The Proper Connective

Now that you have worked with the concepts of coordination and subordination, let us return for a closer look at connectives. You will recall that early in this chapter we discussed *coordinating* and *subordinating* conjunctions.

The right connective or conjunction can aid the unity of a sentence; the wrong one can often destroy it. Connectives can either reinforce or weaken the grammatical coordination and subordination of sentence elements. Even when all your main ideas are in independent clauses, all your subordinate ideas in dependent clauses or other modifying constructions—even then, connectives can improve or spoil the unity of your sentences. Each of them has one of two purposes: coordination or subordination.

Independent conjunctions and conjunctive adverbs are used to show the proper coordination of ideas. If two main statements are written in one sentence, you should join them with an independent or *coordinate* conjunction (*and, but, yet, or, nor,* and *for*) or with a conjunctive adverb (*however, moreover, furthermore, consequently,* and so on). Remember that these conjunctions cannot be used interchangeably. They do not have the same meanings. You must choose the one that exactly fits your intention.

Here are some examples of the effect of several coordinate connectives. A definite topic sentence is followed by four sentences covering about the same material. Each sentence is compound; that is, it has two independent clauses. Each sentence uses a different coordinating connective to join the two independent clause ideas.

TOPIC SENTENCE: **The coast of Maine lies open to the ravages of the weather.**

1. Hurricanes, roaring up from the south, hit in late summer, *and* Atlantic storms lash it in winter.
2. In the course of three months a hurricane may roar up from the south, *or* an Atlantic storm may lash it from the coast.

3. Hurricanes roar up from the south with enough power to destroy light shipping and summer camps along the beaches, *but* Atlantic storms, whipped by furious gales, lash everything before them with great fury.

4. Lately, hurricanes have roared up from the south in late summer, and Atlantic storms have lashed it in winter; *consequently,* many an old resident has chosen to spend his or her last years in quieter areas.

Although similar, these sentences demonstrate the difference in meaning or emphasis that a connective can express. In sentence 1, *and* makes it clear that two things are meant—hurricanes and Atlantic storms. Sentence 2 uses *or* to suggest an alternative—either a hurricane or a storm, not both. Sentence 3 is similar to 1 in talking about both kinds of storms; however, the connective *but*, which here suggests contrast, emphasizes the severity of the Atlantic storms. Sentence 4 makes the storms equal parts of one idea and expresses the consequences by means of the second clause, introduced by *consequently.* The connective *therefore* would also have been possible.

Not all sentences are or should be composed of only independent clauses. In trying to impress the reader that our ideas have different values, we use both coordinate conjunctions and subordinate (or dependent) conjunctions. In addition to subordinating the clause they introduce, subordinating conjunctions often express a much more definite relationship between ideas than coordinate conjunctions do. Some common relationships signaled by subordinating conjunctions are those of *time, cause, condition,* and *concession.* Some common examples are

- *Time:* after, before, when, while, since, until
- *Cause:* because, since, as
- *Condition:* if, unless
- *Concession:* although, even though

Of these relationships, *time* and *cause* are easy enough to understand. *Condition* applies to statements that are true only under certain circumstances, which the dependent clause states: *If we had drilled one foot deeper,* we would have struck oil. *Concession* refers to dependent clauses that seem to be contrary in meaning to the statement made in the independent clause: *Although the poem brought him fame,* it brought him little money.

Notice that *while* is listed only among the connectives expressing time relationship. Most properly, *while* means "time during which." However, *while* is often used in the sense of *although: While he really preferred the sports car,* he knew he should buy the sensible sedan. This use of *while* for *although* is acceptable to most people, but some careful writers avoid it. There is another use of *while,* to mean *and.* Since many people object to it, you should avoid it:

- Hurricanes hit the coast in summer while forest fires destroy timber in at least three seasons. [*And* is better.]

In the following paragraph notice how each of the conjunctions is used:

Sam Beaudine was in a constant state of fret. He objected to the kids *who* shouted at play in the stockade; *moreover,* he growled at the whimpering dogs, straining at the ends of their chains. He sniffed the night air *and* said it carried smoke—Injun smoke. He would walk a spell, bed down a spell, *and* walk again throughout the night. *When* the first soldier straggled back from the ambush, Sam rubbed his beard *and* wiped his brow, *but* he only muttered strange sounds. All that week *and* all the next he grumbled, mumbled, *and* just walked. Then one morning, just before dawn, he heard the horses whinny, *and when* he went to them he found a Comanche arrow buried deep in the roan's neck. At that moment the fretting of Sam Beaudine stopped, *for* he let out a yell *that* could be heard as far away as Laramie, *if* anyone had been listening. The Indians certainly heard it; *furthermore,* they did something about it. *As* the sun rose, the cries of the Indians could be heard from the hill, from the plain, from everywhere, it seemed. *And* Sam, *who* had known all along *that* the varmints were coming, grabbed his gun, began swearing like a sergeant, *and* mounted the walls of the stockade. *While* the powder and bullets lasted, the men kept their guns hot, *but* by midafternoon the ammunition was gone *and* half the men were dead. It was only a matter of time.

Coordination and Subordination in the Paragraph

The principle of coordination and subordination applies not only to the sentence. It plays a role in the paragraph as well. In the sentence, as we have just seen, main ideas belong in independent clauses; subordinate ideas belong in dependent clauses, or other modifying constructions. Ideas of equal importance belong in the same type of grammatical construction. A sentence of two or three equally important ideas would be constructed as a compound sentence. Each independent clause would be equal in basic value to the other. Thus the three independent clauses would be coordinate as grammatical constructions; and the idea expressed in each clause would contribute an equal share to the total thought of the sentence. On the other hand, a sentence of only one main idea and one subordinate idea would be expressed in a complex sentence.

In a paragraph it is generally true that major supporting statements are coordinate, and minor supports are subordinate. (We are talking here of values, not independent and dependent clauses.) Thus in a paragraph of ten sentences, five sentences may be major supports and five (one for each major) may be minor supports. The major supporting statements will be coordinate with each other and the minor supports will be coordinate with each other, but each group will be subordinate to their respective major. To this degree the sentences of a paragraph bear a similar relation to the independent and dependent clause-ideas of a sentence.

¶ Exercises

A. In this exercise you are given a topic sentence and a series of numbered groups of ideas. Copy the topic sentence and underline the controlling idea, and for each number write the group of ideas as one sentence. Apply the principle of coordination and subordination. Put main ideas in independent clauses and subordinate ideas in dependent clauses or other modifying constructions.

TOPIC SENTENCE: **An educated man should have certain skills.**

1. An education should teach a person one important skill, which is the recognition of humbug. The world today is full of empty prizes. Every voter, reader, and television fan should be skeptical of them.

2. An uneducated man's mind chugs along like a barn-built truck. It lacks grace and style, such as the educated man needs in his written prose and in the self-expression that is his speech.

3. Most people use many words when a few will do, because they never learned the art of brevity.

4. Students today grow up reading comic books, which do not contribute much to their prose style. They should develop a good style by constantly reading and listening to the classics and to much good poetry. For a well-tuned phrase and a good prose rhythm are distinguishing traits of the educated man.

5. The art of self-expression has been weakened by school tests that require only the circling of numbers. Instead, the student needs training in giving mind and pen free play.

B. Consider the first sentence of the following paragraph the topic sentence. The rest of the sentences have been divided into thought-units, each one separated by an ellipsis (. . .) and numbered. Copy the topic sentence and underline the controlling idea. Then list the numbers and identify their respective units as "main ideas" or "subordinate ideas." Finally, rewrite the paragraph so that the sentences show good coordination and subordination of ideas.

The gentle art of fishing is not without frustrations. [1]You have waited a long time . . . [2]and you finally have a day off . . . [3]and you drive fifty miles to a lake . . . [4]when you find you left the worms and live bait at home . . . [5]The shoreline is rocky . . . [6]so there are no worms to be had . . . [7]You have no bait net . . . [8]so you can't get more live bait . . . [9]Three precious hours have passed already . . . [10]The sun is getting high . . . [11]and the fish go deep in the lake . . . [12]You are forced to still-fish against your wishes . . . [13]Fruitless hours pass . . . [14]You recall that the weatherman predicted a cool, cloudy day . . . [15]while you suffer increasing pain from the searing sun . . . [16]You rummage through your tackle box for soothing ointment . . . [17]only to find the tube empty . . . [18]You settle down determined to endure all for just one fish . . . [19]Suddenly a violent thunderstorm with driving rain breaks over the lake . . . [20]You remember that being on open water at such times is dangerous . . . [21]so you head for shore . . . [22]and your oar breaks . . . [23]You stand up to paddle the mile to shore . . . [24]The bottom of the boat is covered with water . . . [25]you slip . . . [26]falling overboard . . . [27]You struggle, finally getting back into the boat . . . [28]although you have lost your pole . . . [29]At long last you make the dock . . . [30]discovering that your

leg is scratched and your wrist sprained . . . [31]You repack the car
. . . [32]realizing the whole day has profited you nothing.

C. Select one of the following topics and limit it to a paragraph of about
100 words. Write a topic sentence with a definite controlling idea, and
underline the controlling idea. Include in the paragraph four simple
sentences and six complex sentences. In each simple sentence have at
least one minor supporting idea, properly subordinated, and underline
it. In each complex sentence express at least one minor supporting idea
in a dependent clause and underline it.

1. Killing Time between Planes at an Airport

2. Misleading TV Commercials

3. The Value of Curiosity

4. The Pressures on an Outstanding Athlete

5. Seatbelts Save Lives

6. If Only Management Would Listen

D. A topic sentence is given below, followed by five sentences. Write each
numbered sentence applying the rules for proper subordination.

TOPIC SENTENCE: Primitive peoples were superstitious.

1. The Roman legions conquered England, where they found a people who
worshipped trees and stones.

2. The Aztecs, who were sun worshippers, lived in Mexico long before the
coming of Cortez.

3. Far across the ocean lived the natives of India, who thought the cow was
sacred.

4. In the mountains and remote valleys of many countries the inhabitants,
because they remain superstitious, believe in ghosts, evil spirits, and
spirit voices.

5. South Sea Islanders are also found to be superstitious since they make
wide use of charms—a special stone, a tail of a snake, the gruesome
head of an enemy.

E. Compose a topic sentence on a topic of your choice. Develop its controlling idea by writing five compound sentences that use coordinate connectives (independent conjunctions and conjunctive adverbs). Underline each connective. Then add a dependent clause to each independent clause in the five sentences. Underline each dependent connective. Check over your paragraph to see that it has unity and that you have applied the principles of proper coordination and proper subordination.

4. Paragraph Coherence

Paragraph coherence is really a matter of presenting ideas in a logical and intelligible way to the reader. Achieving unity in a sentence or paragraph is a process of *elimination;* coherence is a process of *organization.* Therefore, at this point, we can see an overall process emerging. Consider these steps:

1. The writer develops a *controlling idea;* that is, what he or she wishes to write about.

2. Having developed a controlling idea, the writer develops a *topic sentence* to serve as a vehicle in the paragraph for the controlling idea.

3. Next, the writer makes a list of *major* and *minor supporting statements* that appear to support the controlling idea.

4. Each supporting statement is then *tested* as described in previous chapters to ensure that it is in unity with the controlling idea.

5. Finally, all of the supporting statements are logically *organized* into a coherent order or sequence.

It may seem contradictory, but it is true, that a paragraph can be unified but not coherent.

Coherence in a paragraph depends upon the correct sequence of sentences, but it also depends upon properly connecting them. To achieve the correct sequence, you should arrange your sentences in the sequence that will most successfully transfer your thought to the mind of your reader. To achieve proper connection, you should provide within individual sentences the guides or aids of reference that will keep the thought of the paragraph flowing clearly from beginning to end, from sentence to sentence, and through each individual sentence. These aids are like highway markers that keep the traveler on the right route. They are discussed in the latter part of this chapter; the first part will deal with the sequence or order of ideas in the paragraph.

Coherence is a major consideration in the revision of a paragraph. If you have, say, five sentences, you must decide which one should come first, which last, and which ones in the middle.

First of all, keep in mind that *basic materials* (details, reason, illustrations) and paragraph *form* (order or sequence of the sentences) are not the same thing. They do, however, act together to make a paragraph coherent. Your basic materials are like the unorganized parts of a parade gathering at the back where it is being formed. These bands, floats, troops of horses, and the like are only potentially a marching column formation. Until they are put into order according to some purposeful pattern, the parts do not make a parade, only a mass of confusion.

The nature of your available materials and your governing intent will influence the pattern of your paragraph. If the controlling idea and the basic materials suggest, for example, that the details, reasons, or illustrations happened chronologically—that is, in an order of time development—the paragraph will probably be written in that sequence. If the controlling idea and basic materials suggest a design or pattern in space, such as the layout of an athletic field or of a supermarket or of the stars and the planets in the sky, the arrangement of the sentences in the paragraph will undoubtedly follow space order. That is, you might explain the arrangement of the component parts of your subject; for instance, from left to right, right to left, top to bottom, bottom to top, or in other spatial terms. On the other hand, if neither time order nor space order seems appropriate, the nature of the material may suggest other approaches: beginning with a general statement and developing it with specific supporting statements; or beginning with a series of supporting statements and building toward a final general statement; or arranging the ideas in the order of climax. It is these orders of paragraph development that we want to discuss in the present chapter: time order, space order, general-to-specific order, specific-to-general order, and order of importance.

There are more complex types of paragraph development (including definition, comparison, contrast, and analogy) to be studied in Chapter 6. In the meantime, by studying the forms discussed in this chapter, you will (1) recognize the importance of an orderly arrangement of basic materials in the paragraph, (2) learn how to achieve such arrangements so that you may practice them at once, and (3) make yourself ready, through practice, to use these skills when you write the more complex types of paragraphs.

Order of Sentences

There are various ways of arranging sentences in a paragraph in order to achieve good coherence. The more experienced you become in writing paragraphs, the more you will experiment with ways of your own. Until that time, however, you should practice the methods below.

Time Order

In a paragraph of time order, the events, steps in a procedure, reasons or judgments about a topic expressed at different periods of time, illustrations of happenings or concepts—in fact, any materials that follow one another in a time sequence—are presented in the order in which they occur. When a time-order approach to paragraph organization is called for, it will usually be very clear from the nature of the controlling idea. The following topic sentences and their controlling ideas clearly suggest such development:

- There is only one way to develop photographs successfully.
- Many people did not know of the events that led up to the conflict in Vietnam.
- Before taxiing to the runway for takeoff, the SST has undergone hours of preparation for the flight to London.
- Next, the acidity of the solution must be determined.
- The Employee Relations Committee was called to order at 10:00 A.M. in Conference Room 8.

Notice that in each of the examples above a time order is either stated or implied. The last example may seem a bit strange, but it could be the first sentence of the minutes of a meeting in which points of discussion are recorded in sequential order.

Here is a paragraph of instruction, in which the writer uses details to explain how to grow a cactus from a shoot. Notice that there is simply no way other than time order to do so.

Cactus propagation is easy. Some varieties of cactus produce miniature offshoots at the base of the parent plant. Remove the little plant, let it dry, then pot it in a sandy medium. If the plant is a branching type, remove a joint; otherwise, cut off a portion of a leaf or stem.

Allow the joint or cutting to dry in a shady place for a few days to a week or more until a callus forms. Then place the cut side down in moist sand or vermiculite. Cover it with a plastic bag and keep it at about 75° F. The rooting medium should stay barely moist—too much water causes rot. When roots have formed, pot the cutting in a sandy soil mixture. [31]

Changing Times

After collecting and studying statistics relating to the atomic bombing of Hiroshima, the writer of the next paragraph presented details chronologically. The time order begins with the exploding of the bomb. Then follows destruction in various forms as people die, buildings cave in, people are injured, fires spread, and more people die. The details of the aftermath are presented as they occurred, with some facts not being fully clear until the present day.

The destructiveness of the atomic bomb is something we have gradually come to realize. We know what it can do from the small 20-kiloton bomb dropped at Hiroshima, which in one split second took 70,000 civilian lives (many more if we include the Japanese soldiers in nearby military installations). Of another 70,000 who were injured, many died later, and others continue to die to this day. The bomb itself did not kill all these thousands directly—that is, through thermal radiation which burns people into charred corpses, or through blast shock which kills in the same way a truck would, in striking down pedestrians in the street. A great many people who were in steel and concrete buildings were killed by walls and roofs caving in on them, or by fires from burning buildings, exploding gas mains and boilers. Those who were injured but still alive under the rubble could not escape the raging fire-storm which followed the blast and finished what was left of them and of the city. [32]

VIRGINIA SNITLOW   "The Mushroom Cloud"

In the next paragraph Samuel Eliot Morison explains how William H. Prescott, the famous American historian, went about the process of writing a book. The "real business" of his working day is presented in illustrations arranged chronologically, with a reason added here and there for the reader's fuller understanding of the historian's creative process.

Returning from his walk at one P.M., Prescott began the real business of the day. The secretary read aloud from memoirs and other documents pertaining to the book then being written, Prescott interrupting frequently to dictate notes or to discuss the persons and events described. After all sources for the chapter at hand had been gone through, the secretary read aloud repeatedly the notes he had taken, and was often called upon to reread some of the sources. This process went on for days. Prescott was then ready to compose. He outlined the entire chapter in his mind, sometimes while sitting in his study, but more often when walking or riding. He wrote the first draft very rapidly on his noctograph. The secretary numbered each sheet as it was finished and copied it in a large, round hand so that Prescott could read it himself. His memory was so remarkable that he could commit a chapter of forty or fifty printed pages to memory, mull it over on horseback, and decide on alterations and improvements. He would then dictate to his secretary the changes to be made in the manuscript and have the whole reread to him. Finally he dictated the footnotes. [33]

SAMUEL ELIOT MORISON   "Prescott, The American Thucydides"

¶ Exercises

A. Assume the following topic sentence is to be developed in *time order* with detail and illustration as the basic material. Supporting materials that might be expanded and included in the paragraph are numbered and listed below. Copy the topic sentence, underline the controlling idea, in parentheses after the topic sentence write "time order," and then list the *numbers* of the items in their proper chronology.

TOPIC SENTENCE: **For hours before its scheduled 8:00 A.M. departure for London, the Concorde was the object of the attention of many people.**

1. The night before, within seconds after the last westbound passengers had debarked, the plane had been refueled.

2. At 6:30 A.M., the pilot and copilot had arrived to begin their preflight check-off procedure.

3. The passengers were called for loading at 7:30 A.M.

4. The baggage handlers waited for last-minute passengers to check in.

5. Every effort is made to assure that the plane will leave on time.

6. The flight attendants carefully checked the cabin to satisfy themselves that the cleaning crew had done a good job.

7. The ground crew had many specialists, who arrived at different times.

8. Two technicians worked through the night to correct a minor problem, one discovered during the flight from London, with one of the radios.

9. Aside from the baggage, the inflight meals were the last to be loaded aboard.

10. With two red batons, the line chief gave the pilot the all-clear sign.

11. At the ticket counter the passengers checked their luggage and received their seat assignments.

12. The flight engineer signed for the fuel.

13. As the passengers boarded, the engines were quietly humming.

14. The eastbound flight crew boarded the van for the trip to the airport at 6:00 A.M.

15. At precisely 8:00, the Concorde was pushed backwards and away from the loading ramp by a tractor.

B. The following paragraph was originally written in *time order* and then scrambled. Copy the topic sentence, underline the controlling idea, and list below it the *numbers* of the sentences in what you consider to be the proper time order.

TOPIC SENTENCE: None of us will forget that November day when Hurricane Daisy roared up the East Coast. [1]Nevertheless, the weather people kept a close watch on it. [2]While there was a sigh of relief in Florida, warnings were going out in the coastal Carolinas. [3]It soon appeared to be heading northwest and intensifying. [4]This time she headed due east. [5]Then, just before going ashore in Florida, she changed her mind and headed off in a northeasterly direction. [6]On Cape Hatteras people headed for public shelters. [7]Again Daisy changed her mind. [8]It was sighted as a minor disturbance just east of Cuba. [9]Now more resolute, she stayed her course. [10]Only six hours after being sighted, Daisy was designated a hurricane, and the residents of the east coast of Florida were warned to take precautions. [11]Losing her strength, Daisy died several hundred miles out in the Atlantic Ocean.

C. Write a paragraph developed by time order on one of the following:

1. Planning a trip just for enjoyment
2. Getting an automobile ready for winter
3. Before the brush even touches canvas, elaborate preparations must be made.
4. What happens before the play opens
5. My personal five-year plan

Space Order

In a paragraph developed by means of space order, the writer arranges material, which will usually be details, according to a predetermined pattern. That is, they are laid out as if pinned to a drawing board. They may be fixed in various orders: from near to far, from high to low, from side to side, whatever pattern is appropriate. If, for example, you were recounting the details of a trip from New York to Hong Kong by way of Europe, the part about New York should come first, the part about Hong Kong last, and the intervening material would be arranged in the order of the trip eastward; for instance, London, Paris, Rome, Athens, Port Said, and Bangkok.

Since each place visited comes later than the previous one, you may think that the paragraph belongs to development by time order. But the point to remember is that in time order *time* is the chief concern of the writer—*when* a place was reached, *when* a thing happened or should happen. In *space order,* space is the chief concern—where each place was located in relation to other places discussed. The "when" is incidental.

In the next paragraph, Rachel Carson, who has made a special study of the sea, illustrates in spatial relationship the movement of the waves from the Atlantic to Lands End, England. Notice that in her topic sentence she mentions both the starting point, "distant places of the Atlantic," and the ending point, "Lands End."

As the waves roll in toward Lands End on the western-most tip of England, they bring the feel of the distant places of the Atlantic. Moving shoreward above the steeply rising floor of the deep sea, from dark blue water into troubled green, they pass the edge of "soundings" and roll up over the continental shelf in confused ripplings and turbulence. Over the shoaling bottom they sweep landward, breaking on the Seven Stones of the channel between the Scilly Isles and Lands End, coming in over the sunken ledges and the rocks that roll out their glistening backs at low water. As they approach the rocky tip of Lands End, they pass over a strange instrument lying on the sea bottom. [34]

The Sea Around Us

Besides giving details in spatial relationship, a paragraph by a gifted writer like Joseph Conrad may include imagery to create a mood that gives further meaning to the basic material. In his short story "The Lagoon," two men are traveling in a boat to the hut of the Malayan, Arsat.

The creek broadened, opening out into a wide sweep of a stagnant lagoon. The forests receded from the marshy bank, leaving a level strip of bright green, reedy grass to frame the reflected blueness of the sky. A fleecy pink cloud drifted high above, trailing the delicate colouring of its image under the floating leaves and the silvery blossoms of the lotus. A little house, perched on high poles, appeared black in the distance. Near it, two tall nibong palms, that seemed to have come out of the forests in the background, leaned slightly over the ragged roof, with a suggestion of sad tenderness and care in the droop of their leafy and soaring heads. [35]

"The Lagoon"

The next paragraph explains in a simple way what could be a difficult problem in surveying if the surveyor had only a carpenter's square and a long measuring tape. The writer not only uses illustration as his basic material, but also supplies line drawings for further clarification. Each action in the procedure of laying out the foundation of the building is—in fact, must be—performed in space order. As you read the paragraph and check what is said with the line drawings, you should know that the author, earlier in the article, made one stipulation: the knots in the rope (Figure 1) must be tied so that the segments are in the proportion of 3:4:5; that is, they may be 6 ft., 8 ft., 10 ft., or 9 ft., 12 ft., 15 ft., or 12 ft., 16 ft., 20 ft., and so on. Figure 2 illustrates how the rope is formed into the triangle that provides the structural design for one-half of the proposed building.

Picture a scene in ancient Egypt thousands of years ago. An Egyptian surveyor, or *harpedonapta,* is walking toward the site chosen for the Pharaoh's next great palace. Following him are three slaves, one of them carrying a rope that is divided into three sections by two knots.

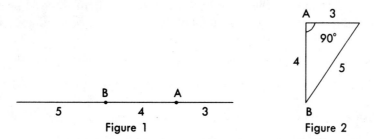

Figure 1   Figure 2

The surveyor marks out one line of the foundation of the building and stations a slave at one end of this line. This slave holds the rope at the point we have marked *A.* A second slave gathers both ends of the rope and walks along the line marked out by the surveyor until the shorter end in his hands is stretched taut. Still holding both ends of the rope, he puts his hands down on the line. The third slave now takes hold of the rope at the point marked *B* in our figure, and walks away from the line until the whole rope is tightly stretched. As if by magic the rope takes the shape of a right triangle with the right angle at the point where the first slave is stationed.[36]

ALFRED HOOPER   *Makers of Mathematics*

The use of space order is not limited to the Conrads or Carsons. The opportunity to use it may be closer at hand than you think. For example, if you are assigned a topic like the following, the material of your paragraph would probably call for spatial development.

- The opening position of chess pieces
- The floor plan of your house
- The setup of an herb garden
- A dress pattern
- The evening weather report
- The shortest route from New York to Chicago

¶ Exercise

Write a paragraph in which you describe a room of your own choice. Make note of the position of doors, windows, pictures, furniture, rugs, or other features that you think appropriate. Your topic sentence should include a controlling idea such as "The living room of our home is a warm, comfortable place."

General-to-Specific Order

The paragraph of general-to-specific order requires less rigid control over materials than paragraphs using the other types. The ordering qualities are present, however, even though subtle, and a recognizably faulty order will disturb a reader. In general-to-specific order, also known as deductive order, the topic sentence and controlling idea make the general statement. The body of the paragraph is composed of details, reasons, or illustrations. The writer may arrange supporting materials so that the most important comes last, the next most important first, and the rest come between in any order he or she chooses. This type of paragraph development is probably most often used by students.

Legend has played an important part in the development of literature. The following paragraph cites a number of legends associated with the biblical Joseph. The author has arranged details in general-to-specific order.

According to Eastern legend, Joseph's feats were many and marvelous. One of the least of these was the gift of tongues: he spoke seventy-one languages. He founded the city of Memphis, and constructed a canal at Cairo for the discharge of the Nile's waters. The mighty pyramids were his handiwork, built as granaries for the storing of grain during the seven lean years. He was the Hermes of Egypt: to his ingenuity the world is indebted for the science of geometry, and for the first system of weights and measures. The use of papyrus for writing purposes was his discovery. He was one of the greatest of the interpreters of dreams. And finally, he was buried in the Nile so that his bones might bless its waters. Though these legends had their origin in the East, most of them found their way to Europe during the Middle Ages. [37]

FREDERICK E. FAVERTY   *Your Literary Heritage*

The writer of the following paragraph combines details and an illustration in general-to-specific order to support her topic sentence.

> The state is a rough-cut jewel—virtually all mountains. There are West Virginians who brag that if the state were flattened, she'd rival Texas in size. Countless times as I explored her reaches, I would pull to a stop to catch my breath at the forested spectacle. One autumn afternoon as I stood overlooking the New River Gorge, a weathered mountaineer turned to me and asked, "You ever been to the Rockies?" When I replied that I had, he continued proudly, "Well, so have I, and it ain't no prettier than this." [38]

> ELIZABETH A. MOISE   "Turnaround Time in West Virginia"

One American linguist believes that English has reached a standardization in certain forms that will change little in the future. He defends his position with reasons and details—opinions based on his study of the language and on specific examples to reinforce his views.

> In the matter of grammatical forms and arrangements, our language today is far too standardized to permit of much change. It is possible that a few stray levelings may take place *(oxes* and *deers* for *oxen* and *deer,* for instance; or *I heared him* in the place of *I heard him).* But despite the widespread rantings of the apostles of "usage" (however that much-belabored word may be defined), it is not likely that substandard forms will make much headway. The primary reason for this is that such sub-standard forms are normally in the nature of localisms. Such rank atroci-ties as "Them dogs are us'ns," "I seen the both'n of 'em," and "I'll call you up, without I can't" are too localized to survive the impact of schools and TV. The only grammatical changes that have a real chance of becoming part of the standard language are those that have nation-wide currency, such as "It's me," "Who did you see?" and "ain't." Judgment may be suspended for some ignorant uses in sentences like "I should of done it" and "I seen him." [39]

> MARIO PEI "English in 2061: A Forecast"

¶ Exercise

From one of the following topics write a paragraph using detail, reason, or illustration in general-to-specific order:

1. Problems during a gasoline shortage

2. Settling in a small town

3. Accepting another's point of view

4. Voter apathy is growing

5. You can't teach an old dog new tricks

Specific-to-General Order

This order of development (also known as inductive order) reverses that of the general-to-specific, and tends to increase reader suspense because the general statement comes *last* in the paragraph; the specific materials are presented one by one to lead up to the general statement. In other words, the topic sentence with the controlling idea is the final sentence of the paragraph. In the general-to-specific order the topic looks forward to the material that is to come; in the specific-to-general order the topic sentence looks backward to material already presented.

In the following paragraph, for instance, the writer, a famous educator, carefully prepares for a distinction between experience and educational training, which is stated in the final sentence.

> Young people do not spend all their time in school. Their elders commonly spend none of it there. Yet their elders are, we hope, constantly growing in practical wisdom. They are, at least, having experience. If we can teach them while they are being educated how to reason, they may be able to comprehend and assimilate their experience. It is a good principle of educational administration because a college or university has a vast and complicated job if it does what only it can do. In general education, therefore, we may wisely leave experience to life and set about our job of intellectual training.[40]
>
> Robert M. Hutchins   "What Is a General Education?"

The subject of the next paragraph is presented in three sections, supported by detail, reason, and illustration. The topic sentence with its compound controlling idea comes last.

The great power of today's automobiles and the four- and six-lane highways, together with improvements to the main roads of the nation, invite—nay, challenge—every driver to see just how much his car will do. Even though the national speed limit is established as fifty-five miles an hour, many trucks and passenger cars, especially the compacts, pay little regard to it and zoom by the law-abiding drivers at seventy or even faster. In emergencies a driver traveling at such speeds has little or no control of his car. Young people, on the other hand, probably imitating their older brothers or parents, not only drive at excessive speeds, but also enjoy showing off. They swerve in and out of traffic, drive with one hand, come to screeching stops, race each other along two-lane highways, wave to passers-by, oblivious of approaching cars. Under such conditions accidents are inevitable and pedestrians are in constant danger. Many a driver, moreover, is careless of the safety of others. While speeding or showing off, he does not realize that he endangers both himself and other occupants of his car; he ignores the fact that thin tires or faulty brakes result in blowouts and smashups. The road hog may force another car off the highway, the radio listener may run down a pedestrian, and the driver who continually tries to beat the light or be the first through an intersection poses a perpetual threat of injury to people on foot who have as much right to cross the street as he has. Thus, increasing numbers of accidents on highways today are due to speed, aided by high-powered motors and disregard for law, to unconstrained youth having its fling, and to everyone's disregard for everyone else.

The next paragraph presents a number of conditions that would exist if one large city in the United States were hit by nuclear weapons. Then the topic sentence, dramatically placed last, implies the tremendous devastation and general chaos that would result if bombs and missiles were to fall simultaneously across the face of the nation.

If New York City were bombed, one could write off the people buried under the rubble. No one could get in to the burning ruins of the city for several days. The surrounding areas would be so occupied by their own efforts to keep alive that they could supply little if any assistance. Eventually, highly trained rescue teams might be able to come from distant areas. These would require, according to technical government bulletins, the following equipment: airplanes or helicopters with survey meters to chart the contaminated areas and direct operations, bulldozers, trucks, fire hose and pumping machinery (since water pressure would be gone), radio receivers and senders, helmets, goggles, breathing filters, dosimeters, geiger counters, uncontaminated food, water, and medical supplies. With a good part of our nation organized to assist, as in cases of storm and flood, something might be done for survivors fifteen or twenty miles from the blast center. However, New York would be, in case of war, only one of many target cities destroyed. The bombs and missiles would be falling all over the United States at about the same time, with each area an autonomy of chaos. [41]

VIRGINIA SNITLOW   "The Mushroom Cloud"

¶ Exercises

A. List five ideas that you might use in a paragraph developed by specific-to-general order for the following topic sentence, which would be placed last in the paragraph:

At last Finley stood poised, one arm up and one foot bare, waiting for the whistle for the kickoff.

B. Write a paragraph using specific-to-general order for one of the following, which may be used as a topic sentence:

1. Times have changed; so now let the *seller* beware.
2. It had become apparent that our business would need a computer.
3. Clearly, success in sewing depends on thorough preparation.
4. We found that energy-saving measures do work.
5. Looking back, Henderson felt that indeed his college education had paid for itself.
6. Necessity is the mother of invention.
7. Something had to give!
8. It is the squeaking wheel that gets the grease.

Order of Importance

The paragraph of climactic order arranges its basic materials from least to most important. This technique is effective because the reader is given information upon which he or she can better perceive the final climactic statement. It is not unlike the technique used in drama and fiction. The paragraph that follows gives reasons for the rapid growth of Paris in ascending importance.

> Three factors contributed to the population explosion in Paris from 1851 to 1872, when the number of Parisians nearly doubled—from 1,242,000 to 2,212,000. The increase was the result partly of better health conditions (the cholera epidemic of 1830 had claimed 1,000 victims a day). The increase was also due in part to the general peace and prosperity of the Second Empire. But the city's population rise came about mainly because the railroads carried the promise of Paris to rural France. Paris grew because it was the only city in France where anyone could arrive and know he could at least survive, perhaps prosper. [42]

> Adapted from Sanche de Gramont   *The French: Portrait of a People*

Anyone who wants to comprehend what is going on in the sciences in the space age must have some knowledge of mathematics. To make his point, the writer of the next paragraph breaks mathematics into component parts and concludes with a reason.

> Our whole modern civilization is built on mathematics! Not a street can be laid, a foundation dug, or a building constructed, without the use of algebra, geometry, and trigonometry. Not a machine can be designed, an engine's performance predicted, an electric power plant constructed, without mathematics through calculus. And the design of an airplane, a ship, a guided missile, or an electronic computer requires a profound knowledge of higher mathematics. No one, in short, from a grocer's clerk to the nuclear physicist can do without mathematics—and the study of mathematics can be a great adventure in the methods of quantitative thinking which will provide a lifetime of better understanding of a technological world. [43]

> Lee DuBridge   "Science—The Endless Adventure"

The following paragraph illustrates climactic order based on opinion. James B. Conant, a distinguished American educator, expresses his opinion first and then quotes that of another person to support his controlling idea.

> The enthusiastic spectators at school and college contests rarely realize how corroding is the spirit generated by their zeal for winning teams. One has to visit high school after high school, as I have done in recent years, to see how much the public is to blame for some of the troubles that plague our public schools. Time and again, at the end of a visit, after discussing curriculums and teaching problems, the superintendent would say to me, "We haven't yet talked about my chief problem, which, to be quite frank, is the record of the high-school teams. Let's face it—what this city demands is that I get coaches whose teams will win, or out I go." [44]

> "Athletics: The Poison Ivy in Our Schools"

In these paragraphs, each of which illustrates a possible ordering of basic materials, the chief concern of the writer has been to develop either a time, space, general-to-specific, specific-to-general, or climactic order of importance. The particular order the writer adopts at the start of writing the paragraph is the one that should be followed throughout. Say from the first he or she "feels" that the order should be defined by succession in time, or the focus from general-to-specific, or the process of building up to a climax. But then, in developing the paragraph, the writer finds that material he or she has put into one kind of order (climactic, for instance, or general to specific) falls into another order (time, for instance). There is no reason to be concerned. The paragraph should be planned and written around one of the orders, and if time (which is probably the chief offender) gets into the act, he or she should not worry. The important thing is that the paragraph turn out to reflect the order intended from the start, for the following of that intention may govern to a considerable degree how the writer states the sentences. Under such circumstances, any other order is incidental.

¶ Exercise

Write a paragraph in which details, reasons, or illustrations are developed by order of climax. Here are some suggested topics:

1. The thrill of a big city
2. A passion for neatness

3. The stupidity of the nuclear arms race

4. This coming summer

Reference Guides—Transitional Expressions

To keep your paragraph-idea flowing clearly and smoothly, you should use reference guides as aids for your reader. Most important in achieving coherence of sentences in a paragraph are transitional expressions, a consistent point of view, and proper pronoun reference. We will study each of these matters in turn.

Single words, phrases, and clauses, and even symbols help show the relationship of ideas in successive sentences. They are the bridges that make the progress of thought easy. Use them, when needed, to anticipate an idea already stated. The following lists give examples.

SOME SINGLE WORDS

first	incidentally
second, secondly	however
third	conversely
next	thus
last	also
finally	then
similarly	besides
accordingly	therefore
namely	moreover

SOME WORD GROUPS

at first	in conclusion
at last	another reason
to repeat	in other words
in effect	on the contrary
that is	for example
in summary	now let us turn to

The following two forms of the same paragraph illustrate the roughness of transition when guides are not used and the smoothness of transition when they are. The first example has an almost childish tone to it, and certainly a boring one. Notice that it is really a string of simple sentences. The second example, as well, is comprised of only simple sentences. But with effective transition, it does not give the impression of simplicity.

Without Transitional Expressions

There are reasons why I like to fish. I enjoy the pull of a four-pound bass at the other end of the line. My enjoyment increases if the fish is in the deep waters of the lake. I don't like him close to shore among the weeds. The hope of catching a big one lures me to the less-known pools and the cool waters beneath some underwater rocky ledge. I like to have a well-oiled and smooth-running motor to drive my boat from spot to spot on the open lake. I like the quiet under the open sky away from the weekend campers and two-week vacationers. I prefer the last reason.

With Transitional Expressions

There are three reasons why I like to fish. First, I enjoy the pull of a four-pound bass at the other end of the line. *Moreover,* my enjoyment increases if the fish is in the deep waters of the lake, *rather than* close to shore among the weeds. *Second,* the hope of catching a big one lures me to the less-known pools and the cool waters beneath some underwater rocky ledge. *Still,* I like to have a well-oiled and smooth-running motor to drive my boat from spot to spot on the open lake. *Finally,* I like the quiet under the open sky away from the weekend campers and two-week vacationers. *Of the three reasons,* I prefer the last.

Here is a paragraph using a different type of transitional expression: numerical symbols. The same effect could be achieved using alphabetic symbols.

The fire inspectors finally determined the causes for the complete destruction of the house. (1) It was a small frame dwelling, and its cellar was full of old papers. (2) The first fire company to arrive had been delayed five minutes by a freight train blocking the only road leading to that section of town. (3) When the firemen arrived, they had difficulty removing the cap from the fire hydrant. (4) Even after they succeeded in attaching the hose to the hydrant, the water pressure was so low that the water could not reach the house.

Most magazines articles and newspaper editorials today avoid the formal symbols such as those in the preceding paragraph, although they are frequently used in books, particularly textbooks, where the author wants to stress sections of thought or to emphasize transitions. Instead of symbols, therefore, single words and word groups are more generally chosen. They are less conspicuous, but when used discriminately, they are probably equally successful. Obviously, the overuse of transitional expressions should be avoided. Notice the transitions in the next example.

> When one is speaking to one's family, *for example,* one uses a certain level of speech, a certain diction *perhaps,* a tone of voice, an inflection, suited to the intimacy of the occasion. *But* when one faces an audience of strangers, as a politician does, *for instance*—and he is the most social of men—it seems right and proper for him to reach for the well-turned phrase, even the poetic word, the aphorism, the metaphor. *And* his gestures, his stance, his tone of voice, all become larger than life; *moreover,* his character is not what gives him these prerogatives, but his role. *In other words,* a confrontation with society permits us, or even enforces upon us, a certain reliance upon ritual. [45]
>
> Arthur Miller   "The Family in Modern Drama"

A word needs to be said here about transitional elements linking paragraphs. Although this book so far discusses matters primarily related to the writing of single paragraphs, you must keep in mind that a paragraph will usually function as a unit within a theme, essay, or report, and, therefore, may serve as a bridge between other paragraphs. For this reason we should consider it—only briefly here, however—along with transitional elements.

As a thought should flow smoothly from sentence to sentence, so too it should flow from paragraph to paragraph. The means by which coherence is thus maintained are often the same means used between sentences. In addition, however, a brief paragraph is sometimes needed to provide the proper transition. Such a paragraph may summarize briefly main points just discussed and identify a new line of development about to be taken up; it may indicate that what has just been treated is only one side of an issue and that the other view also needs consideration; or it may convey some similar comment by the writer. For example, here is a transitional paragraph that would serve in a theme on types of paragraph development:

> Simple types of paragraph development involve primarily the arrangement of sentences within the paragraph; for example, *time order, space order, general-to-specific order, specific-to-general order,* and *order of importance.* Now we must examine the more complex types, particularly those of *definition, comparison, contrast,* and *analogy.*

The reader, having read a discussion of the "simple type[s] of paragraph development," is being signaled that now he or she will hear about the more complex types.

The writer of a paper treating the causes and effects of typhoid fever, after discussing the causes, might prepare the reader for the rest of the paper, which will set forth its effects:

> So far we have been concerned only with the causes of typhoid fever. The remainder of this paper will be concerned with its effects.

In an essay seeking to define what a gentleman is, you might provide the reader with certain dictionary definitions of the word, and prepare him or her in the following transitional paragraph for what you plan to say in the rest of the essay:

> Now that the dictionary meanings of *gentleman* have been established, what do today's men and women mean by the word? That is, what do shopkeepers, bankers, travel agents, and teachers think? What do salespersons, secretaries, flight attendants, and spouses of either sex think?

On occasion an effective transitional paragraph may be cast in the form of an illustration that looks both to what has been said and to what is to come.

> What has been said so far about the advisability of looking for safety devices on a used car may have no effect on the man who comes to the car lot with definite preconceptions. The other day a friend of mine who wanted a particular make of car and model went to a secondhand car dealer. In the lot he saw exactly what he wanted—a clean, shiny sports

car with bucket seats and four speeds. He asked about the condition of the brakes, tires, seat belts, and asked also about a padded dash, automatic door locks, and a collapsible steering wheel. Even though the dealer admitted that the brakes needed relining and the tires had gone 20,000 miles, that some of the latest safety features were not a part of the equipment, the general appearance of the car and the main features my friend was looking for took his eye. He bought the car and proudly drove away. My friend's rash method of buying a used car is duplicated by many people, often endangering their future safety.

Transitional paragraphs take many forms. Some are short, some long. Some are well organized and fully developed; some are quite informal, merely indicating that a unit of thought has been completed and a new one is about to begin. The kind of transitional paragraph you decide upon will be determined by what your reader needs to know at a given place in your whole composition.

¶ Exercises

A. Make a list of all the transitional elements in the order that they appear in the following paragraph:

There are several reasons for my collecting ship paintings of the nineteenth century. First, they are, in a sense, pictorial history. They recall a time when ships were the only means of international commerce. Moreover, pictures of the fighting ships of that century remind me of the naval battles that played such an important role in the fate of nations. Another reason is my interest in the ingenuity of the designers and builders of those ships. Interestingly, no two were alike because it was not an age of mass production. Each designer had only two thoughts in mind, speed and size. Actually, some ships were designed for only one purpose, breaking the speed record around Cape Horn to the Far East. Finally, my collection suggests the romance of the sea. For example, there is the sheer grace of the clipper ships, the immensity of sail on the squarerig-gers, and the lethal rows of gun ports on the warships. Additionally, some are painted on the quiet waters of a bay; others are painted in a storm at sea.

B. Write a paragraph in which you use a variety of transitional elements. Underline each one.

C. Write two transitional paragraphs, and before each explain the purpose of it. Remember that a transitional paragraph links what has come before with what is to come next.

Consistency in Point of View

A coherent paragraph maintains a consistent point of view toward its topic. This consistency is achieved through careful attention to person, tense, voice, number, and tone. We will examine each of these closely.

Person

"Person," you will recall, is actually a matter of *three* persons: first, second, and third. *First person* refers to the pronouns, *I, me,* or *my* and *we, us,* or *ours. Second person* refers to *you* and *yours* in either the singular or plural. *Third person* refers to *he, him,* and *his, she, her,* and *hers, it* and *its,* and *they, them,* and *theirs.*

Point of view as to person involves the stance you take toward your material. You may choose to use the "I" or "we" of the first person. This choice is likely to be most appropriate when you are aiming for an informal, intimate effect. In contrast, the third-person point of view suggests an impersonal, objective treatment. It implies that accuracy, authenticity, and judgment lie behind the details, illustrations, or reasons presented. Both first- and third-person points of view have their uses. If you have a choice—that is, if your material can be treated from either point of view—you will be wise to choose the objective, third-person point of view for serious papers and reports, and the more personal first-person for informal occasions. However, try to avoid such artificialities as "It is the opinion of this writer." Another attitude, popular in textbooks, especially in the behavioral sciences, natural sciences, and engineering, uses the "we-you" approach. For example, "*you* have seen one point of view. Now *we* can [or let us] consider alternatives." *We* substitutes for the reader and the author moving over the the subject together. "We-you" is less formal than the third-person approach, yet it is not strictly informal.

Still another possibility, about which there is some disagreement among writers, is the so-called *indefinite you*—the second-person pronoun that is used in the saying, "You can't take it with you." Some writers find the indefinite *you* a good alternative to the stiff-sounding *one.* Others object to the use of *you* unless the *you* is directed specifically to the reader, as it usually is in explanations in text books, such as this one, and similar situations. Before you decide to use the indefinite *you,* or *we-you,* check your instructor's preferences in the matter.

Whatever point of view you choose, maintain it throughout the paragraph. If you start off in the third person, you should not shift carelessly to first or second person.

INCONSISTENT	CONSISTENT
Until students learn to take themselves seriously and to plan their work hours properly, *you* neglect an important part of *your* education.	Until students learn to take themselves seriously and to plan their work hours properly, *they* neglect an important part of *their* education.

Tense

The three basic tenses are *past, present,* and *future.* When you have decided upon a particular tense as the proper location in time for your material, you should consistently use that tense. If your topic sentence shows that you are looking back upon events that have already happened, your time is past. The tense you use throughout the paragraph should show that the action took place in the past and should not change into present tense. Likewise, if you adopt present tense in the topic sentence, you should not slip carelessly into past tense in the rest of the paragraph.

TOPIC SENTENCE: Members of the committee *began* to oppose the chairman. *(past tense)*

SHIFT TO PRESENT TENSE	CONSISTENT PAST TENSE
When he called a meeting on Monday, they gathered to act on the new resolution. Immediately, however, they *begin* to ask about his political activities.	When he called a meeting on Monday, they gathered to act on the new resolution. Immediately, however, they *began* to ask about his political activities.

Voice

You will recall that there are only two voices, *active* and *passive*, and that only verbs have voice. A verb that has a direct object is in the active voice. If the sentence is rearranged so that the direct object becomes the subject of the sentence, it will be in the passive voice. For example,

- Tom kicked the ball. (active)
- The ball was kicked by Tom. (passive)

Both voices have their place. In most writing, however, the active voice is more effective than the passive voice. That is because the active voice, as you can see from the examples above, is more direct. Though there are times when the passive is preferable, an unnecessary shift is often awkward and weakens the force of the sentence. A shift from active to passive is likely to cause other errors: a needless change from the subject about which the writer is speaking or writing, wordiness, and even faulty subordination of ideas.

TOPIC SENTENCE: The heroism of John Paul Jones *inspired* American seamen to imitate his deeds. *(Active voice)*

SHIFT TO PASSIVE VOICE	CONSISTENT ACTIVE VOICE
They fought with courage, they endured many hardships, and he was willingly followed wherever he went.	They fought with courage, they endured many hardships and they willingly followed him wherever he went.

Number

Number, of course, refers to the fact of whether a noun or pronoun is *singular* or *plural;* that is, whether it involves one, or more than one, thing. A proper use of number is usually essential to clarity. If the controlling idea is to be thought of as singular, all references to it in the course of the paragraph should be singular. Likewise, if the controlling idea or a word or idea in a sentence is regarded as plural, all references to it should be plural. Errors in number occur most often when the writer uses a singular subject and a plural predicate verb.

TOPIC SENTENCE: According to the Constitution of the United States, Congress has a variety of powers. ("Congress" as used here is singular.)

SHIFT FROM SINGULAR TO PLURAL	CONSISTENT SINGULAR NUMBER
Congress is able to raise and support an army, but *they* cannot appropriate money for that purpose for a period longer than two years.	Congress is able to raise and support an army, but *it* cannot appropriate money for that purpose for a period longer than two years.

Tone

Although *tone* is not a grammatical entity, it is an integral part of point of view. In essence, tone is a manner of speaking or writing which reflects the attitude of the speaker or writer. Thus, the tone of a paragraph may be friendly or unfriendly, humorous or serious, direct or indirect, even formal or informal. A college prank, for example, may be described in a humorous way by a fellow student who regards it as a harmless escapade. The dean may take a quite different tone in describing it.

The important thing to remember, however, is that your tone should be suitable to your controlling idea, and it should be consistent throughout your paragraph and, usually, throughout a longer piece of writing. Experienced writers may be able to achieve good effects through surprising shifts in tone, but less-experienced ones will do well to avoid them.

In the paragraph that follows, the writer departs from the formal tone of the first sentence by using inappropriate slang.

TOPIC SENTENCE: The musical production of Dimitri Shostakovich can be divided into two periods. (Serious, dignified tone.)

SHIFT IN TONE	CONSISTENT TONE
The first period began in 1927 and lasted until 1936. During his second period, he *took off* for almost two years from the society of *longhairs*.	The first period began in 1927 and lasted until 1936. During his second period, he *withdrew* for almost two years from the society of *serious musicians*.

¶ Exercise

Correct the inconsistencies in the following passages:

1. When one fails to be consistent in point of view, you run the risk of not being understood.

2. That particular secretary of state was a convincing orator, behaved in every way like a statesman, and was a real weirdo.

3. When the professor put the drop on the surface of the water in the beaker, it sank to the bottom and then rises back to the surface.

4. She asked what I thought, and I say that I really don't think much at all.

5. After the team elected its captain for the following year, they all went to the gym for the usual afternoon practice.

6. He catches the fly, rifled it to the second baseman, and was cheered by all in the stadium.

7. Let us next turn our attention to the nuclear arms race. What a foul-up that has turned out to be! The best minds in both governments make pronouncements that you just can't understand. The Soviet Central Committee issues a statement of policy, but they don't really agree on it. Here our Congress passed a resolution criticizing that policy, received the support of the state legislatures, and were praised by the people. Still no one had the foggiest idea of what the resolution really said.

Pronoun Reference

As you begin this section, it may be well to remind you that this book stresses rhetorical principles whose application will help you to write better paragraphs, and to add that it is only collaterally concerned with the problems of pronoun reference within the sentences of a paragraph. Some linguists hold to formal usage in certain instances of pronoun reference; others tend to favor informal usage. At this point you may well wonder just what it is that we are talking about. Briefly, it is this. Grammar is based on rules. One such rule is that a pronoun must be in the proper case for the way that it is used in the sentence. Usage, on the other hand, refers to the way people write and speak regardless of the rules of grammar. You, hearing someone come into your house, call out, "Who's there?" The grammatically correct answer would be "It is I." But in American usage, the answer will invariably be "It's me."

Both formal and informal usage are used by writers, depending upon their purpose, the occasion for which they write, and their projected readership. Most of your paragraphs are related to your courses or occupation and are intended for a teacher or a colleague. Your English usage, therefore, should agree with theirs when they are composing for a similar occasion. Your writing should be neither stiffly formal nor excessively informal. Therefore, you should write the best English you can. Because there are different views about usage, especially about the reference of pronouns, it seems wise to suggest that if you write your own topic sentence, you should follow consistently the point of view, tone, and level of usage established in that sentence.

Usage aside, the very important point for you to keep in mind is that the paragraphs you write should be clear and consistent.

On this theory, then, the following samples and explanations regarding pronoun reference are preceded by a topic sentence that gives you direction for consistent practices. Headings are supplied to indicate what seems to be, and what seems not to be, the preferable usage in sentences that might appear in a paragraph developed from that topic sentence. The term "informal" is used with several samples for alternative choices that appear to be acceptable because they are finding sanction in the writing of reputable authors.

Pronouns (including possessive adjectives) are important guides to the proper relationship of ideas, not only within a sentence but also between sentences in a paragraph. Although correct agreement of pronoun with antecedent within a single sentence is essential to clear writing, the chief interest here is in the coherence that results when a pronoun in one sentence maintains a proper reference to some word in another sentence of the paragraph.

Remember that a pronoun agrees with its antecedent in person, number, and gender. Most errors occur when the antecedent is singular and the pronoun referring to it is plural, or when the antecedent is plural and the pronoun is singular.

In the following paragraph notice the proper use of both pronouns and possessive adjectives to carry the writer's thought from sentence to sentence. To the right of the paragraph, the pronouns and possessive adjectives referring to *Lincoln* and *people* have been listed under their respective antecedents.

	LINCOLN	PEOPLE
Abraham Lincoln rose before the people to deliver the Gettysburg Address. *Some* of the spectators paid little attention to the President. *Others,* more respectful and sensing *his* humility and dedication, fixed *their* eyes intently upon the man standing on the platform before *them. His* tall, gaunt form sagged a little from weariness. *His* eyes patiently and sadly sought out the eyes of *his* audience. Reverently *he* stood in the presence of the buried dead, who but recently had given their full measure of devotion. Tolerantly *he* awaited the quieting of the living. Then, clearing *his* voice, Lincoln began to speak.	his his his his he he his	some others their them

In the above paragraph the problem of reference is rather simple. It involves keeping each of the words *Lincoln* and *people* in clear relationship with the necessary reference words used in the following sentences of the paragraph.

In other paragraphs, however, you often permit faulty references to creep into your writing because you do not express a definite antecedent at all. Such errors are illustrated in the following passages, taken from student papers. The topic sentence is given first; then inconsistent, ambiguous, or informal usages are shown at the left and the preferred form of each pronoun reference is shown at the right, with explanations just below.

TOPIC SENTENCE: From the start of the trial the *jury* was very cautious.

INCONSISTENT	CONSISTENT
Although at times the jury seemed favorably impressed by the prosecution's case, *they* were out four days before bringing in a verdict.	Although at times the jury seemed favorably impressed by the prosecution's case, *it* was out four days before bringing in a verdict.

The predicate verb *was,* in the topic sentence, shows that the writer at the start thought of *jury* as singular: *"it* was."

TOPIC SENTENCE: According to the Department of Athletics, *anyone* who *comes* to the basketball games *is* required to follow the rules set by the Department.

INCONSISTENT	CONSISTENT
They must make *their* reservation in advance.	*He* must make *his* reservation in advance.

The indefinite pronoun *anyone,* and certain others like it (such as *each, one, either, neither*), take singular verbs and singular reference words. Note, too, that one mistake in reference may cause other errors, as in *reservations* for *reservation.* With pronouns *everybody* and *everyone,* singular reference is often preferred, though in informal usage a plural reference is common; for example:

TOPIC SENTENCE: According to the Department of Athletics, *everybody* attending the basketball game must have their own *tickets.* They should present . . .

Most readers would probably be more comfortable reading *"his* own ticket. *He* should present . . ." But many people in formal writing will accept *their* . . . *They* as a tolerable informality.

   Your pronoun, even though it matches its noun in number, may nevertheless be confusing. For example:

TOPIC SENTENCE: At the opening of the concert season last night, the audience felt the masterful control of the conductor.

UNCLEAR	CLEAR
At length the guest artist took his place at the piano and the conductor half-faced him. Then *he* nodded and the Beethoven concerto was begun.	At length the guest artist took his place at the piano and the conductor half-faced him. Then, *after the guest had indicated his readiness, the director nodded* and the Beethoven concerto was begun.

In the passage at the left the pronoun *he* refers ambiguously to either *guest* or *conductor.* To clarify the reference, the identifying clause *after the guest had indicated his readiness* is inserted, and the noun *conductor* is substituted for the indefinite word *he.*

TOPIC SENTENCE: For one reason or another, everyone was interested in Pete Grant, the hero of the Tiger football team.

UNCLEAR	CLEAR
Even Coach Bob Smith did not lose sight of his star until *he* left the campus.	Even Coach Bob Smith did not lose sight of his star until Pete left the campus.

Who left the campus? *He* can refer either to *Coach Smith* or to *star.* The substitution of *Pete* for *he* assures clarity.

TOPIC SENTENCE: All the people living in my block are famous for something.

FAULTY	CLEAR
This is the *man's* house *who* won the state lottery. *He* bought a fifty-cent ticket and won $50,000.	This is the house of the man *who* won the state lottery. *He* bought a fifty-cent ticket and won $50,000.

Faulty reference results when a pronoun is made to refer to a word used as a possessive modifier. In the faulty sentence, the pronouns *who* and *he* refer to *man's.*

TOPIC SENTENCE: Class rivalry at the school was seldom one-sided.

UNCLEAR	CLEAR
Seniors and freshmen often took advantage of each other. *They* hid their class caps so that *they* could not recognize them.	Seniors and freshmen often took advantage of each other. The *freshmen* hid their class caps so that the *seniors* could not recognize them.

Each *they* could refer to either *seniors* or *freshmen.* The vagueness of the reference is increased by the addition of *their* and *them.* Substitution of *freshmen* for the first *they* and of *seniors* for the second *they* clears up the problem.

TOPIC SENTENCE: Frequently, important men in civic offices must give up their duties because of an emergency.

<table>
<tr><td align="center">UNCLEAR</td><td align="center">CLEAR</td></tr>
</table>

UNCLEAR	CLEAR
Only last week the mayor of our city had a heart attack. *It* had been weakened, the doctor said, by overexertion in athletics.	Only last week the mayor of our city had a heart attack. His *heart* had been weakened, the doctor said, by overexertion in athletics.

Here the pronoun *it* is made to refer to *heart attack,* not to *heart.*

TOPIC SENTENCE: People often act without sufficient justification.

AMBIGUOUS	CLEAR
Henrietta accused the teacher of grading on a curve and of being partial to boys. Moreover, Henrietta showed *it* every day in class.	Henrietta accused the teacher of grading on a curve and of being partial to boys. Moreover, Henrietta showed her *resentment* every day in class.

The pronoun *it* is made to refer to an idea implied in the preceding sentence, to an idea that led to the accusation. Since that idea is nowhere represented by a definite word, a word should be substituted for the pronoun *it*.

A frequent ambiguity in reference occurs when a writer uses a pronoun to refer to an antecedent that has not been expressed but has only been implied in a preceding part of the paragraph. Correct the vagueness in one of three ways: (1) use the right pronoun to refer to some word that has been given; (2) express the idea that has been omitted; (3) rewrite the sentence so that the ambiguous reference is removed. The pronouns most commonly involved in correcting such faulty references include *they, it, which, that, this (these), that (those),* and *everybody.* Formal usage requires precise pronoun-antecedent relationships; informal usage permits less precise ones.

TOPIC SENTENCE: Every county in New York State, at least according to the Chamber of Commerce, is famous for something.

INFORMAL

I used to live in Orange County. *They* are famous for dairy cattle.

CLEAR

I used to live in Orange County. *It* is famous for dairy cattle.

or:

I used to live in Orange County, *which* is famous for dairy cattle.

or:

I used to live in Orange County. The *farmers* there are famous for dairy cattle.

or:

Orange County, where I used to live, is famous for dairy cattle.

TOPIC SENTENCE: In recent years the radio, television, and press have given abundant evidence of the declining moral standards of the American people.

INFORMAL

In yesterday's paper it said that juvenile delinquency was a major problem.

CLEAR

In yesterday's paper an *editorial* [or an article] said that juvenile delinquency was a major problem.

In similar sentences, such as those beginning "I read in the paper . . ." and "I saw in an article . . . ," the following usage is not acceptable: "I read in the paper *where* juvenile delinquency . . ."; "I saw in an article *where it said* that . . ." A person can read a statement, an editorial, or a report, but he or she cannot read a *where.* The sentences can be improved thus: "I read in the paper *that* juvenile delinquency . . ."; "An editorial in yesterday's paper claimed that juvenile delinquency . . ."

TOPIC SENTENCE: The American school system continues to be fond of certain anniversaries.

AMBIGUOUS

Historical dates and events associated with the growth of

CLEAR

Historical dates and events associated with the growth of

America are especially popular. The pilgrims landed at Plymouth Rock in 1620, *which* is celebrated in schools everywhere.	America are especially popular. *The landing of the Pilgrims at Plymouth Rock in 1620* is celebrated in schools everywhere.

INFORMAL

Historical dates and events associated with the growth of America are especially popular. The Pilgrims landed at Plymouth Rock in 1620. This is celebrated in schools everywhere.

Although the "informal" reference is acceptable, it is suggested that the student may prefer to use the "clear" sample of reference in order to avoid any possible misunderstanding.

In the following parallel paragraphs, the one on the left illustrates informal usage, the one on the right formal usage. Both are acceptable in modern writing. It should be added, however, that if the words *these, their, it,* and *this* in the informal passage should seem at all vague, you should employ the more precise phraseology of the formal passage.

INFORMAL	FORMAL
When the storm had passed, everything was a shambles [*topic sentence*]. Great elms lay uprooted across streets and lawns. *These* had been the pride of the village fathers. Everybody from the mayor to the garbage collector made *their* way past demolished houses and damaged stores. *It* was an appalling sight. Broken glass was strewn everywhere. House roofs had been blown into the streets or hung dangerously from the top	When the storm had passed, everything was a shambles [*topic sentence*]. Great elms, *which* had been the pride of the village fathers, lay uprooted across the streets and lawns. Everybody from the mayor to the garbage collector made *his* way past demolished houses and damaged stores. The *widespread destruction* was an appalling sight. Broken glass was strewn everywhere. House roofs had been blown into the streets; still others hung

corners of the buildings. *This* caused policemen to put up "No Trespassing" signs in all danger zones.

dangerously from the top corners of the buildings and caused policemen to put up "No Trespassing" signs in all danger zones.

¶ Exercises

A. For each of the numbered sentences in the following passage make a list of all of the pronouns and possessive adjectives that aid coherence.

The salt marsh near here is constantly changing. [1]In the spring there is a day when it seems to regain life after the long winter. [2]Suddenly there is a sound that one cannot but notice. [3]Each of the species that enjoys this special place also has its distinctive place in this sound. [4]There is the whirr of the wings of ducks, not heard during their sojourn in the South. [5]The amphibians emerge from the mud and resume their croaking chorus. [6]The insects, which flit about, each with their characteristic movement, contribute their collective hum to the music of the marsh. [7]The playful otters swim among the new cattail fronds, which produce a swishing sound in the water. [8]The fish are there, silent until one of them breaks the surface in search the flying morsels they seem to fancy. [9]A heron stands in stoic dignity and with what seems like endless stillness, listening and watching, trying to divine what his next meal will be. [10]The sounds will continue, even increase, over the summer as new members of the family are hatched or born; some will never leave the marsh. [11]Others will leave but, with their uncanny sense of direction, will find their way back to the marsh from thousands of miles away.

B. Correct the faulty or unclear pronoun references in the following sentences. Be able to explain all other pronoun references.

1. Where is the man's car who had the accident?
2. Anyone who wants to see the rock group, The Indolence, must get their tickets weeks in advance.

3. Neither my sister nor I were willing to make up.

4. The candidate rose to speak but first shook the hand of the county chairman. It was then that he smiled confidently.

5. In *Sports Illustrated* it says that professional athletes' salaries will be going even higher.

6. The referee tossed the ball up, a guard got the tip-off, and he started running for the end of the court.

7. This is the artist's studio who used to paint here.

8. The mayor and council were in sharp disagreement. They took the view that taxes would have to be lowered.

9. In my hometown, they are never satisfied with the performance of the police.

10. The district attorney came down hard on crime, which was the best thing he ever did.

5.
Sentence
Coherence

A coherent sentence is one that is integrated, consistent, and intelligible. Although there are usually fewer elements to keep straight, coherence is important in sentences as well as in paragraphs. Since sentences are the stuff that paragraphs are made of, their effectiveness determines how well the paragraph will succeed in the view of the reader. Like the weakest link in a chain, a poorly written sentence can seriously impair a paragraph which contains otherwise good sentences. The improper placement of a modifier; a faulty relationship between ideas; the omission of needed words: these and other common errors can hinder the smooth flow of thought from the beginning to the end of a sentence.

There are three basic problems that we must examine in order to achieve sentence coherence: the faulty use of modifiers, faulty parallelism, and omissions.

Faulty Use of Modifiers

A *modifier* is a word or group of words that limits or clarifies the meaning of another word. Confusion may result if the modifier is incorrectly placed or if there is no word in the sentence for it to modify. Before going on, let us take a brief look at just how modification works. Some words standing alone have little if any meaning. Take, for example, the word "automobile." Immediately upon reading the word, your mind starts the modification process and you give "automobile" a context. You may think of *your* automobile or one *that you would like to have.* In both cases the italicized words are modifiers. The modification of words is not only useful but essential to the writer.

Misplaced Modifiers

As a rule, a modifier should be placed as near as possible to the word modified. If it is put near some other word that it *could* modify, the coherence of the sentence is likely to suffer. For example:

- *Shining in all its glory,* John watched the rising sun.
- The big rock fell as we rounded the cliff *with a tremendous thud.*
- The committee that investigated the petition *yesterday* gave its report.

In the first of these sentences, the italicized modifier seems to say that *John* was "shining in all its glory," but the meaning is certainly that the *sun* was *shining.* The sentence would be clear if the modifier followed *sun.*

In the second sentence, the cliff could not possess a "tremendous thud"; neither could we "round" with "a tremendous thud"; therefore, the phrase should be placed near "fell," the word with which it really belongs.

In the third sentence, the reader wonders whether the committee "investigated the petition yesterday," or whether it "yesterday gave its report." The sentence is simply not clear.

A word, phrase, or clause used in such a position that it can look forward as well as backward is called a *squinting* modifier. To correct such a modifier, either place it in another part of the sentence, near the word it really modifies, or leave it where it is and add a clarifying word to the remaining part of the sentence—or else revise the entire sentence. For example: "The committee that investigated the petition gave its report *yesterday*"; or, "The committee that investigated the petition *yesterday* gave its report today"; or, "The committee, *after investigating the petition yesterday,* gave its report."

In the following paragraph the thought that develops the controlling idea is broken by misplaced modifiers, which have been italicized in the faulty version. An improved version is given for comparison.

FAULTY	IMPROVED
The circus offered the youngster something new every minute. The Midway echoed the loud,	The circus offered the youngster something new every minute. The Midway echoed the loud,

ceaseless chatter of the barkers. *Walking a tightrope and juggling a bamboo pole,* one of the barkers pointed a stick upward toward the sky and called attention to the "Amazing Ugolino." The boy moved on toward the menagerie tent. Going in he found it lined with animals from every part of the world. He stood fascinated by an elephant balancing a pole *with peanuts in one hand and* an *ice cream cone in the other.* A moment later he watched a sleeping monkey, *wide-eyed,* as it hung by its tail. When the main event was about to start, one barker *just* reduced tickets for his sideshow five cents, but the youngster entered the main tent instead of buying one. On his way home he decided that the Wild West Show was the most exciting event *which came right after the main show* in the whole day's attractions.

ceaseless chatter of the barkers. One of the barkers pointed a stick upward toward the sky and called attention to the "Amazing Ugolino," walking a tightrope and juggling a bamboo pole. The boy moved on toward the menagerie tent. Going in he found it lined with animals from every part of the world. With peanuts in one hand and an ice cream cone in the other he stood fascinated by an elephant balancing a pole. A moment later, wide-eyed, he watched a sleeping monkey as it hung by its tail. Just when the main event was about to start, one barker reduced tickets for his sideshow five cents, but the youngster entered the main tent instead of buying one. On the way home he decided that the Wild West Show, which came right after the main show, was the most exciting event in the whole day's attractions.

Of course, misplaced modifiers are easier to overlook in your own sentences than in examples in which they are italicized. If you are in doubt about where to put a modifier, try reading the sentence slowly, aloud if possible. After each noun, pronoun, or verb, repeat the modifier until you locate the word with which it makes the best sense. For instance, in the third sentence of the preceding faulty paragraph, the position of the phrase "walking the tightrope" makes it modify "one" (of the barkers), but obviously the barker was not on the rope. The Amazing Ugolino was. Thus the modifying phrase goes with "Amazing Ugolino." In the sentence about the peanuts, the pole could not hold the peanuts and the ice cream cone, but "he" could. In this particular instance, the sentence sounds smoother if the phrase is placed first. In the sentence about reducing the price of tickets, the meaning seems to be that the reduction occurred "Just before" the start of the main show. The misplaced adverb "just" belongs in front of "when" instead of in front of "reduced." In the last sentence the adjective clause does not modify "event." It modifies "Wild West Show."

As we have suggested, reading your sentence, aloud if possible, may help you to see, or even hear, the faulty use of a modifier. Another trick is to analyze each sentence by circling each modifier and drawing an arrow to the word or words modified. The longer the arrow, the greater is the chance of the faulty use of modifiers. For example:

- Shining in all its glory, John watched the rising sun.
- John watched the rising sun shining in all its glory.

Dangling Modifiers

A *dangling modifier* is one which has *no* word in the sentence to modify. For example:

- Sailing into New York harbor, the Statue of Liberty was a thrilling sight.

A dangling modifier usually creates a ridiculous, even comic, image which is likely to distract your reader from what you are saying. The modifier in this example is "Sailing into New York harbor," but notice there is nothing to indicate *what* or *who* was sailing into the harbor. At any rate, it certainly was *not* the Statue of Liberty.

How do such sentences come to be written? They usually result from the omission of a self-evident but necessary part of the message. The example above seeks to combine three ideas:

- We were sailing into New York harbor.
- We saw the Statue of Liberty.
- It was a thrilling sight.

Even though the first of these sentences has been reduced to a participial phrase in the example, the writer has the original subject (We) so firmly in mind that he or she assumes it is still in the sentence. The key, of course, is "we." There are several ways to improve the example:

- Sailing into New York harbor, *we* were thrilled at the sight of the Statue of Liberty.
- As *we* sailed into New York harbor, the Statue of Liberty was a thrilling sight. [Correct but awkward]
- As *we* sailed into New York harbor, *we* saw the Statue of Liberty, a thrilling sight. [Less awkward]

You will recall that an active-voice verb has a direct object; a passive-voice verb does not. Another frequent cause of dangling modifiers is the use of a passive construction, which displaces the subject (of the active sentence) that the phrase modifies:

- Entering the room quickly, the police found the corpse. [active voice] Entering the room quickly, the corpse was found. [The change to passive voice causes the modifier to dangle.]
- To play tennis, a person needs a tennis ball and racket. [active] To play tennis, a tennis ball and racket will be needed. [The change to passive voice causes the modifier to dangle.] With sentences of this kind, the dangler can usually be corrected if the passive voice is changed to active voice.

The most frequent dangling modifier in student sentences is the verbal phrase (participle, gerund, or infinitive phrase). It usually comes at the beginning of a clause, although it may come elsewhere. At the head of a clause it dangles because the subject of that clause is not able to do what the verbal phrase says. With few exceptions, the following rule will help you to correct such dangling verbal phrases. *The subject of the clause in which the verbal phrase is used as a modifier should be able to do or to be what the verbal phrase says.* Recall a previous example: "Entering the room quickly, the corpse was found." The word "entering" certainly implies that *something* or *someone* entered the room. The corpse was already there!

A word of caution: correcting a dangling modifier hastily or uncritically may lead you into another dangling construction. For instance, notice carefully each version of the idea in the following:

WRONG:　　*After hearing the alarm,* the clock was turned off.

STILL WRONG:　　After *his* hearing the alarm, the clock was turned off.

After *John's* hearing the alarm, the clock was turned off.

After hearing the alarm, *John's* clock was turned off.

IMPROVED:　　After hearing the alarm, *John* turned off the clock.

After *John* heard the alarm, *he* turned off the clock.

John heard the alarm and turned off the clock.

So far, the examples of dangling modifiers have been in single sentences taken out of context; that is, in sentences separated from the paragraphs in which they belong. When dangling modifiers occur in paragraphs, and are not detected in revision, coherence suffers. Carefully note the faulty and improved paragraphs that follow. The faulty version contains dangling modifiers in italics; in the improved version these have been corrected.

FAULTY

Nancy, our old horse, shied at everything. *With a blind right eye* unexpected sounds on her right side terrified her. *Ambling along Mill Road one day,* a squirrel screeched suddenly just above her head and sent her down the road in front of a cloud of dust. Not five minutes later, *while watching a fisherman pull in a fish* and, therefore, *not watching where we were going,* the horse slipped into a small chuckhole, became startled, and was off again. There was another time *when only fifteen,* I remember it well. We were driving into Sugar Loaf. *Deserted, except for three empty buckboards lined up at the general store,*

IMPROVED

Nancy, our old horse, shied at everything. With a blind right eye, she was unable to see half the world, and unexpected sounds on her right side terrified her. As she was ambling along Mill Road one day, a squirrel screeched suddenly just above her head and sent her down the road in front of a cloud of dust. Not five minutes later, while I was watching a fisherman pull in a fish and, therefore, was not watching where we were going, the horse slipped into a small chuckhole, became startled, and was off again. I remember another time when I was only fifteen. We were driving into Sugar Loaf. On the main street,

Nancy was very much alone. *Jogging along half asleep—* she knew every step by heart—a lone puppy, barking and wagging its tail furiously, tore out of a side yard. Up on her hind legs went Nancy, pawing the air in front, and then, *whinnying in fright,* the wagon and I were off through the village lickety-split.

deserted except for three empty buckboards lined up at the general store, Nancy was very much alone. As she was jogging along half asleep—she knew every step by heart—a lone puppy, barking and wagging its tail furiously, tore out of a side yard. Up on her hind legs went Nancy, pawing the air in front, and then, whinnying in fright, she took the wagon and me off through the village lickety-split.

Modifiers Indicating Faulty Subordination

A careful writer avoids ending a sentence with a verbal phrase introduced by "thus" or "thereby." For example:

TOPIC SENTENCE: Mike Brown, the field-goal specialist, was the hero of the game.

- He kicked the field goal thus *winning the game.*

As an idea in a paragraph, "winning the game" is probably more important than "kicking the field goal." The sentence, therefore, illustrates weak subordination. Correct it by subordinating the idea of "kicking" or by making it equal to the idea of "winning."

- *By kicking the field goal,* he won the game.
- He *kicked the field goal* and won the game.

Avoid expressing the really important idea of a sentence in a verbal phrase.

¶ Exercises

A. Correct the following sentences, which contain misplaced modifiers.

1. Because I helped her with her homework last evening, she baked me a cake.

2. Rising out of the waters of the Atlantic, the new day dawned with the sun.

3. Key West is south of Miami, which is the very southerly end of Route 1.

4. Running across the lawn and into the woods, I saw a beautiful deer.

5. I put my goods for sale on the racks, which I had already tagged.

6. I milked the cow sitting on the three-legged stool.

7. The adventurer told us how he had crossed the ocean in the auditorium.

8. Yelling "full speed ahead," we had to admire the courage of the captain.

9. Elm Street will be closed all week for repairs to motorists.

10. Kicking and screaming, Professor Hall led the physics department into the nineteenth century.

B. Correct any dangling modifiers in the following sentences.

1. Landing out of a thick fog, we were amazed at how smooth it was.

2. Putting the dishes in the sink, the meal was over.

3. Hurrying to save time, the shortcut was taken by Ed.

4. Cruising up the Hudson River, the George Washington Bridge was indeed an imposing sight.

5. Eating his lunch, the worm can was opened in preparation for the afternoon's fishing.

6. Having finished the hem, the dress was done and ready to wear when the occasion arose.

7. He had rolled, mowed, and raked the lawn, thereby calling it a day.

8. Baked in an oven for eighteen minutes at 450°, mother served the best biscuits you'll ever eat.

9. Wanting desperately to pass the exam, the long hours of studying were well worth the effort.

10. Washington, D.C., is a city well worth seeing. Strolling up the Mall, the dome on the Capitol seems to get larger and larger. Entering the Lincoln Memorial, the Great Emancipator sits in stern silence. Going on to the wax museum, the curator told us how the figures were made. Upon

entering the Smithsonian Museum of Science and Technology, the flag that inspired the national anthem hangs in a conspicuous place. In front of it, swinging to and fro, the attendant explained the pendulum that never stops. While going on a tour of the White House, the President was in the Oval Office meeting with one of his advisers. Wanting to see everything, the Mall was crossed time and time again. So impressive was the sense of history that we got, the bus ride back home was uneventful.

Faulty Parallelism

Sentence elements that are similar in form and function are said to be *parallel.* By form we mean the grammatical construction of the element, that which defines the word, the phrase, the clause as such. By function, we mean the element's grammatical use in the sentence; for instance, whether it comes into play as a subject or a predicate. Compound subjects and compound predicates are two obvious examples of parallel structures:

- *Jim* and *Wendy* went to Cleveland. [compound subjects]
- They *went to Cleveland* and *visited friends.* [compound predicates]

Phrases and clauses of equal form and similar function should also be parallel:

- The woman *wearing the large hat* and *carrying the briefcase* is the new mayor.
- *If the car is repaired by Friday* and *if the roads are clear of snow,* Jan will drive us into the city.

As a rule, two or more ideas equal in value are coherently expressed in similar grammatical constructions: two subjects, two predicate verbs, two complements, two adjectives, two adverbs, two prepositional phrases, two dependent clauses, two independent clauses. Usually, parallel ideas are joined by the coordinating conjunctions *and* or *or* (or some combination of these words, such as "not only . . . *but also,*" "both . . . *and,*" "either . . . *or,*" "neither . . . *nor*").

Notice how the following italicized words, phrases, and clauses are expressed in parallel form.

George and *Sue* bought tickets to the game.	Noun parallel with noun (also subject parallel with subject)
On the hillside were *tall* and *stately* pines.	Adjective parallel with adjective
The deer raced *swiftly* and *easily* through the woods.	Adverb parallel with adverb
The boys raced *through the house* and *up the stairs.*	Prepositional phrase parallel with prepositional phrase
Victory depends upon three things: *stopping the enemy, cutting off his reinforcements,* and *destroying his supplies.*	Verbal phrases parallel with each other
If Middletown wins or if Central High loses, we shall have the title.	Dependent adverbial clause parallel with dependent adverbial clause
He prostrated himself in the dust before his Maker, but *he set his foot on the neck of his king.*	Independent clause parallel with independent clause
I bought not only a *house* but also a *car.*	Noun parallel with noun
Either *your brother goes with you* or *you stay.*	Independent clause parallel with independent clause

Faulty parallelism results when ideas that are equal and that should be expressed in parallel form are not written in parallel form. For instance, if you have two equal ideas and express one as an independent clause and the other as a dependent clause or a phrase, you are probably guilty of faulty parallelism. Since the independent conjunctions *and* and *or* are used not only with ideas of the same value, but also with grammatical constructions of the same kind, you must not use them to link ideas or constructions that have unequal values in rank, quality, or significance.

In the chart on page 120 are examples of ideas that are equal in value but that are not in constructions of equal value. Occasionally, you may have just the opposite situation. You may have in a sentence ideas that are not

FAULTY:	As a son of Secretariat, the colt was	*of good stock* *and* *valued greatly.*	Prepositional phrase parallel with verb
IMPROVED:	As a son of Secretariat, the colt was	*of good stock* *and* *of great value.*	Prepositional phrase parallel with prepositional phrase
FAULTY:	*I shot a large buck* *and* *it was dressed* on the spot.		Active voice parallel with passive voice
IMPROVED:	*I shot a large buck* *and* *dressed it* on the spot.		Active voice parallel with active voice
FAULTY:	*Condemned by the court* *and* *since he was also denied a new trial,*	he faced death.	Verbal phrase parallel with dependent clause
IMPROVED:	*Condemned by the court* *and* *denied a new trial,*	he faced death.	Verbal phrase parallel with verbal phrase
FAULTY:	*To play baseball* *or* *going fishing*	is my preference.	Infinitive phrase parallel with gerund phrase
IMPROVED:	*To play baseball* *or* *to go fishing*	is my preference.	Infinitive phrase parallel with infinitive phrase
FAULTY:	Her voice was	*clear* *and* *with resonance.*	Adjective parallel with prepositional phrase
IMPROVED:	Her voice was	*clear* *and* *resonant.*	Adjective parallel with adjective
FAULTY:	*Fred Astaire danced in many musical shows* *and* *which were great hits*		Dependent clause made parallel *with independent clause because of and*
IMPROVED:	*Fred Astaire danced in many musical shows* *which were great hits.*		Ideas probably not equal; delete *and*

120

equal in value but that are put in grammatical forms that are equal. For example:

The grizzly bear had $\left\{ \begin{array}{l} \textit{brown eyes} \\ \textit{a black nose} \\ \text{and } \textit{three cubs.} \end{array} \right.$

The three nouns *eyes, nose,* and *cubs* are not of the same value. The first two name physical parts of the bear, the third one, *cubs,* does not. Since the third idea is not related to the first two ideas, it should be separated from the others.

The grizzly bear	had brown eyes and a black nose.
She	had three cubs.

The proper order of the parts of a sentence is essential to its clarity. If in the process of revision you fail to correct misplaced modifiers and faulty parallelism, you set up unnecessary obstacles to the progress of your thought.

¶ Exercises

A. Correct the faulty parallelism in the following:

1. There are two types of guitar players, the strummers and those who pick out melodies on their strings.
2. Not only the hunters but also those who were the hunted were slowed up by the dense fog.
3. It is not unusual to have doubts about a new teacher and having a new experience to look forward to.
4. Our talk was of an interesting nature and enjoyed by both of us.
5. Ted Williams was an excellent hitter, fielder, and played for the Boston Redsox.
6. To study or playing touch football isn't much of a choice.
7. We are going to have a winning season, we are going to qualify for the tournament, and winning it will make us champions.

8. The couple had a son, a daughter, and a shiny new car.

9. David Appleby is a good judge and who treats those who come before him with respect.

10. The panther is strong, fast, and is dangerous.

B. Rewrite the following paragraph so that equal ideas are expressed in parallel form.

The stadium during Superbowl was a very busy place. On the field, in the stands, and broadcasting from the press booth, all was in motion. Of the players not on the field, some performed calisthenics, others played catch in back of the bench, and moping with their heads in their hands. In the bleachers the fans shouted, waved their arms, and a few didn't even seem to be very interested. The vendors rushed up and down stairs to sell hot dogs and pouring soft drinks. Several bands were playing different songs and to cheer the teams on. The officials were comical as they rushed about the field, throwing their flags, and dived into the mass of bodies to get the ball where it was downed. Both coaches were both big, tough-looking, who intently studied the play before them.

Omissions

A sentence may lack coherence because you omit words needed for grammatical completeness or completeness of thought. Frequently the omitted word or word group is in your mind, but you fail to write it down. Most errors of omission occur because you leave out of a sentence one or more of the following:

1. A noun idea

2. A preposition that belongs in an idiom

3. A part of a predicate verb

4. The dependent conjunction *that*

5. The article *a, an,* or *the,* especially when an article is needed to make an identification

6. A word needed to complete the intensives *too, so,* or *such*

7. A word needed to complete a comparison

Here are examples of each type of error. For each one you will find the following: first, the topic sentence of the paragraph from which the sentence is taken; second, asterisks (***) in each faulty sentence to identify the place where the omission occurs; third, a corrected version. The faulty sentence is placed at the left, the improved sentence at the right.

Omission of a Noun Idea

TOPIC SENTENCE: **The condemned man narrowly escaped the gas chamber.**

FAULTY	IMPROVED
Finally, the governor signed the stay of execution with very little *** to spare.	Finally, the governor signed the stay of execution with very little *time* to spare.

Omission of a Preposition That Belongs in an Idiom

TOPIC SENTENCE: **I never knew a good teacher who did not have the welfare of her students at heart.**

FAULTY	IMPROVED
As a rule, she is interested *** and sympathetic toward the on-the-way-to-school problems of each one.	As a rule, she is interested *in* and sympathetic toward the on-the-way-to-school problems of each one.

Omission of a Part of a Predicate Verb

TOPIC SENTENCE: **In my opinion, cheerleading is a most important activity.**

FAULTY	IMPROVED
Cheerleaders always have *** and always will do their best to	Cheerleaders always have *done* and always will do their best to

stimulate enthusiasm at the
games.

stimulate enthusiasm at the
games.

Omission of the Conjunction that *(needed to avoid misreading)*

TOPIC SENTENCE: The attorney for the defense was making a good case for his
client.

FAULTY	IMPROVED
The office manager reported *** the error by the bookkeeper had been corrected before the state auditor arrived.	The office manager reported *that* the error by the bookkeeper had been corrected before the state auditor arrived.

Omission of an Article *(needed for separate identification)*

TOPIC SENTENCE: The governor's latest appointments, as well as his past ones, have
been based upon merit.

FAULTY	IMPROVED
He appointed to the Smithers Committee the mayor of the city and *** former FBI agent for Clark County.	He appointed to the Smithers Committee the mayor of the city and *the* former FBI agent for Clark County. [Two persons appointed]
	or,
	He appointed to the Smithers Committee the mayor of the city, who was a former FBI agent for Clark County. [One person appointed]

Omission of Words Needed to Complete Intensives

TOPIC SENTENCE: In the summer of 1950, the United Nations' forces in Korea were
on the defensive.

FAULTY	IMPROVED
At first the supply line was too inadequate***.	At first the supply line was too inadequate *to permit an advance.*
Later, they had to retreat so far south ***.	Later they had to retreat so far south *that there was danger of their being pushed into the sea.*

The simpler way to deal with this error is to delete the intensive. Thus: "At first the supply line was inadequate." "Later, they had to retreat far south." But if the writer originally wants to intensify the ideas of "inadequate" or "far south," he or she needs to complete the intensive expression.

Omission of Words Needed to Complete Comparisons

TOPIC SENTENCE: **The eyesight of birds is important to their livelihood.**

FAULTY	IMPROVED
It is only natural that the vision of the hawk must be sharper than *** a robin.	It is only natural that the vision of the hawk must be sharper than *that* of a robin.
	or,
	It is only natural that a hawk's vision must be sharper than a robin's.

TOPIC SENTENCE: **Mt. Everest is one of the natural wonders of the world.**

FAULTY	IMPROVED
It is higher than any *** mountain known to man.	It is higher then any *other* mountain known to man.
	or,
	It is the highest mountain known to man.

TOPIC SENTENCE: **Florence Nightingale was one of Britain's greatest women.**

FAULTY	IMPROVED
She was one of the most famous ***, if not the most famous, nurse in the Crimean War.	She was one of the most famous *nurses,* if not the most famous, in the Crimean War.
	or,
	Of the nurses in the Crimean War, she was one of the most famous, if not the most famous.

Numerous Omissions

Here is a complete paragraph with various omissions. The faulty version contains the errors, the improved version is a correction, and the suggested improvements are italicized.

FAULTY	IMPROVED
Summers was an odd one all right. He was up regularly at 6:15 in the morning, left his apartment at 6:40 on the dot, and on the bus two and one-half minutes later. On the way downtown he never looked nor talked with anyone, though he traveled with the same people week after week. He had such an inferiority complex. At 7:06 he arrived at the automat where he always had, and presumably always would eat his breakfast, at least as long as he worked in shirts at Bernstein's. While getting his change for a quarter he said good morning to the coin manager and assistant manager—always he figured a little monologue under the	Summers was an odd one all right. He was up regularly at 6:15 in the morning, left his apartment at 6:40 on the dot, and *was* on the bus two and one-half minutes later. On the way downtown he never looked *at* nor talked with anyone though he had traveled with the same people week after week. He had such an inferiority complex *that he could not force himself to be even mildly sociable, except for business reasons.* At 7:06 he arrived at the automat where he always had *eaten,* and presumably always would eat his breakfast, at least as long as he worked in shirts at Bernstein's. While getting his change for a quarter he said good morning to the

circumstances might make them notice him. Moving on, he pushed coins into the slots in the glass-eyed wall, turned knobs, and had delivered a sticky bun from a swinging door that almost clamped shut on his right-hand fingers and a cup of coffee and cream from an exasperating spout that never, never overflowed his cup. The place was so busy. Then he looked everywhere for a seat, alone. Finally he edged himself in beside three fat mutes who merely slopped their bun and coffee mechanically. At exactly 7:28 Summers rose out of his chair, slid his leg round it, and headed for the swinging door. As he looked about, he realized he was one of the loneliest, if not the loneliest, man in New York.

coin changer and *the* assistant manager—always he figured a little monologue under the circumstances might make them notice him. Moving on, he pushed coins into the slots in the glass-eyed wall, turned knobs, and had delivered a sticky bun from a swinging door that almost clamped shut on his right-hand fingers, and a cup of coffee and cream from an exasperating spout that never, never overflowed his cup. The place was so busy *that* he looked everywhere for a seat, alone. Finally he edged himself beside three fat mutes who merely slopped their *buns* and coffee mechanically. At exactly 7:28 Summers rose out of his chair, slid his leg round it, and headed for the swinging door. As he looked about, he realized he was one of the loneliest *men* in New York, if not the loneliest.

¶ Exercise

Supply the words needed for grammatical completeness or completeness of thought. (The insertion of omitted elements may require a slight revision of the sentence for idiomatic or conventional form.)

1. Many a driver has, and will continue to take, unnecessary chances on the highway.

2. Once he had received his degree, he applied and accepted a teaching job at Wentworth High.

3. More cab drivers drive Plymouths than any kind.

4. When all the money had been collected, it was found to be too little; so the chairman announced that the committee would try again.

5. Inspiration is at heart of all creativity.

6. In New England the weather is as cold as parts of Siberia.

7. A certain busybody who lives on our street is always prying, even lying about the affairs of the neighbors.

8. Summers we spend trying to make enough for fall tuition.

9. I been wondering about my future.

10. Pete Rose, the manager and first baseman of the Cincinnati Reds, attended the baseball managers' convention in Chicago. It lasted as long or longer than usual.

6.
Complex Methods
of Paragraph
Development

The development of a paragraph may be thought of as simple or complex. Simple types of development were discussed in Chapters 1 and 2; that is, paragraphs developed by details, reasons, or illustrations—or by a combination of these methods. In this chapter, we will examine the more complex methods. Although various names have been given to specific types of paragraph development practiced by experienced writers, we are here interested in four that you are likely to use most often; namely, *definition, comparison, contrast,* and *analogy.*

The complex method of development you should use will be determined primarily by your purpose with regard to your basic materials. For clarifying the meaning of something, you would use *definition;* for showing the similarities between persons, places, or things, you would use *comparison;* for showing the dissimilarities, you would use *contrast;* and for suggesting a similarity of relationships among sets of things, such as heart-to-body and engine-to-auto, you might use *analogy.*

When the topic sentence calls for one of the complex methods of development, you should keep two principles in mind. The first is *unity.* If your purpose is to define, then the controlling point of view for admission of material into the paragraph must be *definition;* that is, every detail, illustration, or reason that you use must contribute to that definition. Everything else must be omitted. On the other hand, if your purpose is to compare, only such basic material as contributes to that *comparison* may be included. This same principle—strict adherence to unity—also applies to paragraphs of *contrast* and *analogy.*

The second principle to keep in mind is *order.* In Chapter 4 we considered five primary orders: *time, space, general to specific, specific to general,* and *climactic importance.* In any of the complex methods of paragraph development you should determine which arrangement of details, reasons, or illustrations will be most effective. Suppose, for example, that your purpose is definition of a word like *honor.* You might decide to define it by stating and illustrating the various concepts of honor held by people throughout the ages. You could arrange these illustrations or examples in time order.

At first glance, such a paragraph resembles any paragraph you might have written as an assignment at the end of Chapter 2. There is, however, one very important difference: everything that goes into the paragraph defining *honor* is governed by the purpose of the paragraph—namely, definition. Paragraphs of comparison, contrast, and analogy, likewise, have their own specific governing principle.

To achieve the interweaving of specific purpose, basic materials, and appropriate order, something new is added to the obligation of the writer. It might be called an additional kind of supervision. Heretofore, you might have written a paragraph on the topic sentence, "According to the Chamber of Commerce, Allendale offers many inducements to industries interested in locating branch plants and offices in the Midwest." Your problem in writing such a paragraph would have been a relatively simple one: you merely break down the concept of "inducements" into its component details, put them in an appropriate order, and exclude all extraneous material.

But suppose that your topic sentence is worded this way: "Allendale's civic progress compared favorably with that of Brocton during the period from 1900 to 1920." Now you would have to keep clearly in mind not only the statistical details pertaining to Allendale but also those pertaining to Brocton. Furthermore, you must remember that the purpose of your paragraph is a comparison of the two groups of statistics.

Let's carry this procedure one step further. Suppose that you are preparing to write a paragraph comparing the civic progress of Allendale with that of Brocton. The basic material is probably detail. You compose a topic sentence and arrange the supporting details available to you in parallel columns just below. For simplicity's sake, let *A* represent Allendale and *B* Brocton.

TOPIC SENTENCE: **Allendale's civic progress compared favorably with that of Brocton during the period from 1900 to 1920.**

A's population in 1900 was forty thousand.	*B*'s population in 1900 was fifty thousand.

A's population in 1910 was fifty-one thousand.	*B*'s population in 1910 was sixty thousand.
A's population in 1920 was sixty thousand.	*B*'s population in 1920 was sixty-eight thousand.
In 1900 *A*'s city boundaries enclosed fifteen square miles.	In 1900 *B*'s city boundaries enclosed twenty square miles.
In 1920 *A*'s city boundaries enclosed twenty square miles.	In 1920 *B*'s city boundaries enclosed twenty-five square miles.
A had eight industries in 1900.	*B* had ten industries in 1900.
A had twelve industries in 1920.	*B* had fifteen industries in 1920.

The topic sentence and tabulation above suggest how you might proceed in listing your materials, or in thinking about them, before you write. Then, as you compose the paragraph, your details fall easily into time order; *and* you must keep constantly in mind the idea of comparison, for it will influence the way your sentences will go.

Definition

To most of us *definition* means one of two things: either the lexical or precise meaning of a word; or the rhetorical or expository statement of that word's meaning as understood or interpreted by the writer. The first involves little more than a dictionary entry and may be expressed in a single sentence, in a phrase, even in a synonym. The second is what the definer wants to say about a word or idea in a particular context and elaborate upon—in a paragraph or even a full essay. A sentence definition of a word like "galaxy" and "Rump Parliament" may be called for in a work on astronomy or history, respectively; the same could be demanded of "civil rights" in a study of cultural history or political science. In any case, the definition would attempt to provide further clarification of the word or idea. Unless definition makes the subject being defined clearer and more understandable, it fails in its purpose.

A glance at any general dictionary will soon disclose that many, if not most, common words have more than one meaning. Suppose, for example, someone asked you to define what you mean by a *square*. You might have difficulty arriving at an intelligible formulation, unaided. In any event, a definition would require that you put the word in a class having common characteristics and then give the meaning that differentiates it from the other members of its class.

Like many English words, *square* has a number of meanings, depending upon the context in which it is used. Consider these contexts:

- A *square* is a person who is rejected for conventionality or respectability.
- Of the name Mary, George M. Cohan sang that "there is something there/that sounds so square."
- The square of a number is computed by multiplying it by itself.
- The fuzz works for the squares, baby, and you don't dare trust one.

The problem of defining a word is not always an easy one, but the procedure is basically the same. Notice how it is applied to the following words or ideas:

WORD OR IDEA	CLASS	DIFFERENTIATION
autobiography	written account	of a person's own life
sociology	science	dealing with the origin and evolution of society
oxygen	chemical element	that supports combustion
body politic	group of persons	organized for government
school	institution	for teaching and learning

The definition of each of these terms might well be expressed in a single sentence that most people would recognize as its basic meaning.

For words and ideas like *square* and *civil rights,* however, a full paragraph or more may be required for adequate clarification. You might expand the basic meaning, even starting with it, by elaborating the meaning of the word or idea in terms of your own understanding of it. For example, in defining the word *biography,* you might give its precise dictionary meaning—"the written account of a person's life"—and then go on to tell what a biography attempts to do. The writer of the following paragraph starts with the essential dictionary meaning; then he proceeds directly to a summary of what biography means to him. Definition is his overall type of development, reason is his basic material, and general-to-specific order is his arrangement of sentences.

In sum, biography is the reconstruction of a human life. It attempts to describe and evaluate one individual's career, and also to reproduce the image of his living personality, analyzing its impact upon his actions and the world in which he lived. All biographies must be historical and scientific in that they aim at truth and depend upon verifiable evidence. At the same time they must be imaginative and artistic, because insight and felicity of expression are essential if three-dimensional truth is to be transferred to the flat surface of a printed page. The biographer's responsibility is large. He essays the role of a god, for in his hands the dead can be brought to life and granted a measure of immortality. He should, at least, then, seek to emulate the more reliable divinities in his zeal for truth, his tolerance of human frailty, and his love for mankind. [46]

JOHN GARRATY   *The Nature of Biography*

A paragraph of definition may be a serious setting forth of the basic qualities of its subject, developed as a reasoned explanation of what the writer implies in the topic sentence and controlling idea. To the author of the preceding paragraph, *biography* involves description and evaluation, historical and scientific truth, imagination and artistry, insight and felicity of expression, and the other qualities cited. In writing his paragraph, the author covers the basic features of any good biography, so that the reader gets a sense of the subject in its wholeness.

Another paragraph of definition may treat its subject with less completeness but with a lightness of touch. For the occasion it may be sufficient that the author define merely one aspect of his topic, expressing it in the form of illustration. To be successful, however, the illustration should demonstrate the two basic requirements of definition: that the subject be placed in a class having common characteristics and then differentiated from other members of its class. Furthermore, if the tone of the particular piece of writing of which the definition is a part is informal or humorous, that tone should be maintained in the development of the definition.

It seems to be generally taken for granted that wife-beaters are not gentlemen in twentieth-century terms and that self-control is expected of a gentleman, under even the most trying circumstances. A gentleman does not lose his temper so thoroughly that he commits violence, even on a golf course. Profanity may be permissible, even to the clergy, under such circumstances, but no gentleman wraps his number-four iron around his caddy's neck or throws his spoon into the water hazard. Indeed, Nicholas Murray Butler, the late president of Columbia University, said, "One of the embarrassments of being a gentleman is that you are not permitted to be violent in asserting your rights." [47]

RUSSELL LYNES   "Is There a Gentleman in the House?"

The writer of the next paragraph restates in fuller form the classifying and differentiating features that one would find in a dictionary definition of a simile. Notice how the many examples illuminate the meaning of this technical term.

One of the chief kinds of figurative language is the *simile.* A simile is the direct comparison of two objects, qualities, or concepts for the sake of attributing a characteristic of one to the other. A simile is an open or obvious comparison; it always uses the word "like" or "as." (The Latin word, *similis, simile,* means "like" or "as.") Thus, "My love is like a red, red, rose" is a simile; so are "sly as a fox," "slow as Christmas," and "quick as a wink." In every simile, some reasonably tangible action or object (a rose, a fox, Christmas, a wink) is cited for an outstanding quality (beauty, slyness, slowness, quickness), and any object directly compared with one of these (e.g. "my love") is assumed to share that quality. Poets are fond of comparison in a few words. Burns's tribute to his sweetheart asserts that she is beautiful, fresh, young, and sweet-smelling, simply by comparing her to a "red, red rose," which presumably has all these qualities. Properly used, a simile can make many positive comparisons in a few words. [48]

JAMES W. JOHNSON   *Logic and Rhetoric*

Such definitions, as you can see, give more than the minimal dictionary meaning, and more than the textbook definition with which you constantly work in your courses. Although the writer may or may not begin with the precise meaning of the subject, or an amplification of it, he or she further clarifies its meaning by using the basic materials of paragraph development, especially reason and illustration. The purpose is to help the reader understand the word or idea more completely than would be possible from the dictionary meaning alone.

You will have many opportunities to use the one-sentence dictionary definition in class or in papers written for your courses or in the conduct of your business, but there may be times when you must elaborate on the meaning of a word or an idea in paragraph form. You may be required to define *drag racing, literature, skin diving, isotope, gazetteer,* or *concrete.* Consider, for example, the problem of defining or explaining the word *concrete.* When we think of the quality "concrete," we think of something definite or specific, as opposed to something indefinite, general, or abstract. Look up the word *concrete* in your dictionary and compare the meaning given there with that provided by the writer of the following paragraph, which was developed by reason and illustration in general-to-specific order:

> Concrete words are those which are precise and accurate in their meanings. They carry their meaning through sound, feeling, or association. *Smooth,* for example, is a smooth word; say it aloud and see how it slips from your tongue. But harsh, grating *acrid* is not so easy to say. *Hollow* has the sound of a fist beating on an empty barrel. You say *hard,* and your tongue rises to the roof of your mouth to snap off the final *d,* but you pronounce *easy* and the word slides pleasantly between your tongue and your teeth. *Yellow* brings to your mind a vague impression of color, but *yellow as maple leaves in fall* calls up a definite picture. *Cherry-red, apple-red,* and *brick-red* probably evoke pictures for you, while *cerise, carmine, magenta, henna* may mean nothing at all. Speak of the *buzz* of a bee and you are unconsciously imitating the noise of its vibrating wings. Speak of the *rattle* of an automobile, the *clang* of a bell, the *crash* of an accident, the *bang* of an explosion, the *squeak* of a rusty hinge, and you are using words that approximate the sound described. Speak of *tongues* of flame, *box-like* houses, or *rolling* hills, and you have pictured shapes. Write of *apple-red* cheeks, *corn-colored* hair, and *sea-green* eyes, and you have pictured color—and what a combination! Or write of *smooth* pavements *ground* by the *crushing* wheels of a heavy truck, and you have appealed to your reader's sense of touch. For these are concrete words. [49]

> J. Harold Wilson and Robert S. Newdick *The Craft of Exposition*

In the paragraph that follows, the writer sets out to define Harlem, not as a specific place, but as a symbol recognized throughout the world. Notice the progression from general to specific details.

In a very real sense, Harlem is the capital of Black America. And America has always been divided into black and white, and the substance of the division is social, economic, and cultural. But even the name Harlem, now, means simply Negroes (even though some other peoples live there too). The identification is international as well; even in Belize, the capital of predominantly Negro British Honduras, there are vendors who decorate their carts with flowers and the names or pictures of Negro culture heroes associated with Harlem like Sugar Ray Robinson. Some of the vendors even wear t-shirts that say "Harlem, U.S.A.," and they speak about it as a black Paris. In Havana a young Afro-Cuban begged me to tell him about the "big leg ladies" of Lennox Avenue, hoping, too, that I could provide some way for him to get to that mystic and romantic place. [50]

LEROI JONES   *Home*

Of all the words or ideas that one is called upon to define, perhaps the most difficult is the abstract concept, which expresses a quality apart from an object. Words like *honesty, democracy,* and *justice* belong to this class. Even when a meaningful definition is conceived and expressed for such words, many other explanations of its meaning could be formulated that would be acceptable. Of like difficulty are the adjectives formed from abstract nouns. Such a word is *liberal.* Because most of us today are vitally concerned with the kind of education that leads to good citizenship, it seems appropriate to end this section with a definition of liberal as it applies to education. Its author uses reason in general-to-specific order.

Any education that matters is *liberal.* All the saving truths and healing graces that distinguish a good education from a bad one or a full education from a half-empty one are contained in that word. Whatever ups and downs the term "liberal" suffers in the political vocabulary, it soars above all controversy in the educational world. In the blackest pits of pedagogy the squirming victim has only to ask, "What is liberal about this?" to shame his persecutors. In times past a liberal education set off a free man from a slave or a gentleman from laborers and artisans. It now distinguishes whatever nourishes the mind and spirit from the training which is merely practical or professional or from trivialities which are not training at all. Such an education involves a combination of knowledge, skills, and standards. [51]

ALAN SIMPSON   "The Marks of an Educated Man"

¶ Exercises

A. Write a one-sentence definition of each of the following: *ghetto, terrorism, space, ecological, theology, tunnel vision, thrift, political patronage, municipal.* You are likely to benefit from *not* referring to the dictionary.

B. Look up one of the following terms in the dictionary. Then write a paragraph of definition in which you combine the dictionary meaning of the word and what the word means to you: *fortitude, happiness, ripoff, stupidity, professional, decent, parallel, blue, nuclear, dunk.*

C. Read this passage as a paragraph of definition and then answer the questions that follow it.

I caught the disease known to college freshmen as homesickness. Like raindrops forming in a puddle, the causes for my homesickness came one by one. I woke that fateful morning with the symptoms of a head cold. My nose was stuffy, my mouth felt dry, and my eyes were watery. The drizzly weather outside depressed me as I shuffled through the soggy leaves to my 9 o'clock class in Recitation Hall. Mr. Wolfe's lecture dealing with myth in early Biblical stories left me confused, for it contradicted religious beliefs I had cherished since Sunday School days. I found it hard to believe that the story of Adam and Eve was a theological legend; and I couldn't understand how Joseph, Abraham, and Isaac were personifications of tribes. Then, after class, unaware of the sorority period of silence, I felt dejected when upperclass coeds whizzed by me on the campus without their usual smile or friendly hello. Supported by the knowledge that I had studied for eight hours for my western civ exam on the Romans, I eagerly hurried to my ten o'clock class to learn my test result. I was stunned by the "D" scrawled in red ink across my paper. In shame I trudged back to the dorm for lunch. There I found a letter from Mother waiting for me in my mailbox. I tore it open. "Dear Carole," it began, "We all miss you so much." As I read the word "miss," the writing began to blur. I hurried to my room and locked the door. My throat ached and tears filled my eyes. "The house"—the words wouldn't hold still—"seems empty without you." Clutching the letter, I threw myself across the bed and buried my tears in the pillow. [52]

CAROLE MASLEY [A student]

1. Is the term to be defined clearly stated?

2. What is the controlling idea?

3. What is the basic material used?

4. What is the order of development?

5. Does the writer make any specific use of the dictionary meaning of the term being defined?

6. Is the paragraph definition of the word more meaningful than the dictionary definition? If so, why?

7. Is the paragraph effective?

D. For a foreign exchange student or someone who is not familiar with the term being defined, write a paragraph defining one of the following:

barbeque
Equal Rights Amendment   Air Force One
jeep   liftoff

Comparison

Comparison shows the *similarity* between two or more people, places, objects, or ideas. The word itself, "comparison," hints that there are differences as well as similarities to the people, places, objects, or ideas being compared. For example, two red bricks cannot be compared. A red brick and a tan brick could, however, be compared. A comparison can be expressed in a single sentence or expanded into a paragraph. Let's take the case of the single sentence first. If Henry and George resemble each other physically, you might say, "Both boys have similar features." Or, you might say, "New York and San Francisco are flourishing seaports," comparing an important feature of both cities. You can compare *free* and *independent* as words having similar import, for both mean "not subject to the rule or control of another." These are all simple comparisons.

Each of these brief comparisons, however, may be extended into a paragraph of comparison by the use of supporting details, reasons, and illustrations. You might break down the physical characteristics of Henry and George into a number of component likenesses and illustrate several of them in some pertinent way. You might expand your basic comparison of New York and San Francisco as seaports by giving statistics on their respective waterfront areas: number of piers, the shipping tonnage accommodated annually, gross yearly value of imports, accessibility to means of transportation, and so on. *Free* and *independent* may be further explained with appropriate illustrations. For all such comparisons your opinion or evaluation could be included at suitable places in the discussion.

In a discussion a companion may interrupt you with the purely American expression, "You are comparing apples with oranges." A careful writer does not compare things indiscriminately. There must be a *basis for comparison.* For example, in the two preceding paragraphs, *the things compared belong to the same class or group: Henry and George are both boys, New York and San Francisco are both seaports, and "free" and "independent" are both words.* Unless *the basis of comparison is the same,* the resulting comparison will be illogical and ineffective. It simply would not do to say, "New York is a financial center, and San Francisco is a seaport." While the statement is true enough, there is no basis for comparison.

The careful writer of a paragraph, moreover, not only starts with a basis of comparison between the similar things being discussed but also stresses throughout the comparison *the specific dominant quality, point,* or *issue* that *is applicable to both* and that *is stated or implied in the controlling idea* of the paragraph. Let us suppose that you plan to compare the rigorous disciplines maintained at the Military Academy at West Point and the Naval Academy at Annapolis. *The two academies are your basis of comparison.* What you are comparing, a quality common to both schools—that is, the limited area of interest for this particular paragraph—is the rigorous discipline maintained at each place. *Discipline, then, becomes the controlling idea.* As you compose this paragraph, you must keep constantly in mind that everything you say about discipline must concern not only rigor but also be applicable to both schools. You must also exclude from the paragraph everything that does not contribute to demonstrating some similarity of discipline at both academies.

In the following paragraph Clifton Fadiman draws a comparison between Byron and Hemingway. His primary purpose is to show that both men had similar personality traits and similar experiences, although they were born about a hundred years apart. Fadiman's paragraph, which occurs in an essay, lacks a topic sentence; however, he prepares for the paragraph in the discussion that leads up to it. A topic sentence has, therefore, been supplied in brackets.

[Byron and Hemingway, strangely enough, are somewhat alike in personality and experience.] [1]Both Byron and Hemingway awake to find themselves famous at twenty-five. [2]Both cut themselves off at an early age from their native lands. [3]Byron adopts Greece and Italy; Hemingway celebrates Spain. [4]In Greece Byron finds the fatal theater in which to stage his worship of liberty. [5]In Spain Hemingway discovers the shrine for his cult of violence. [6]Both are attracted by the glory of military life, and meet with disillusion. [7]Both are highly prepossessing examples of maleness and both exploit an athleticism which wins for them—as much to Byron's satisfaction as to Hemingway's disgust—a matinee-idol popularity among literary young ladies. [8]Both are attracted to wild and romantic places—Byron to the Swiss mountains and the Greek coast, Hemingway to Montana and the Ozarks. [53]

"Ernest Hemingway: An American Byron"

With a proper basis of comparison and a controlling idea that establishes the specific quality, point, or issue to be applied to the subjects being compared, you may draw for supporting statements on details, reasons, or illustrations, singly or in combination. When you come to this point in your composition, you are also concerned with expressing your basic materials in the form of major and minor supports. Each major support should be relevant to *both* objects of the comparison and to the controlling idea as well. Each minor support should be clearly related to its major statement and the controlling idea as well.

Let us apply what has just been said to the paragraph about Byron and Hemingway, the sentences of which are numbered for easy reference. The topic sentence with its controlling idea suggests a comparison between two famous writers who resemble each other in personality and experience. The supporting material, in summary form, is identified below as major or minor, and is given the number of the sentence in which it is used in the paragraph. Several explanatory comments are also given.

TOPIC SENTENCE: Byron and Hemingway, strangely enough, are somewhat alike in personality and experience.

1.   *Major:* Both writers are famous at twenty-five.
2.   *Major:* Both men cut themselves off from their native lands.
3.   *Minor:* Byron went to Greece and Italy; Hemingway went to Spain.

(One statement for each man. The desire of both men to become identified with some new place finds fulfillment in experience. Thus the major statement and the controlling idea are properly supported.)

4., 5.   *Minor:* Both find release for their energies in foreign lands. The cause of the release is different for each man, but the important thing is that both men find it. The writer used one sentence for each statement, but both sentences serve the same purpose.

6.   *Major:* For both men a military life leads to disillusion.

7.   *Major:* Their maleness attracts ladies to both, although with different results. However, the attraction is the main point. (Note that the difference in result is introduced parenthetically and could be omitted.)

8.   *Major:* The same kind of landscape appeals to both men.

The Byron-Hemingway paragraph is both unified and coherent. It is unified because all the sentence-ideas develop the similarity between the two men in terms of the controlling idea. The major statements support the controlling idea directly; the minor statements support the major statements and the controlling idea as well. At the same time, all the sentences are written with careful attention to proper coordination and subordination of ideas. The paragraph is coherent because it follows a predetermined general-to-specific order of materials, and because the writer uses within the sentences such transitional units as *both, their,* and *in Greece.*

A paragraph of comparison may be developed by means of detail, reason, or illustration, alone or in combination. In a paragraph using detail you might compare two athletes like Willie Mays and Arnold Palmer, who rose to the heights of their respective professions and gained the admiration of sportsmen everywhere. Ignoring all their differences, you would stress only those qualities possessed by both that contributed to the success for which they are admired. You could include: both are called "real pros"—keen, objective students of their trade; both have cool nerve, a perfect sense of timing, and an instinct to do the right thing at the right time. Other paragraphs of comparison using detail as the basic material could be written on the challenge provided by two golf courses or two mountain peaks, the ultimate objectives of two teachers or two politicians, the scenic pleasures of two highways, or the satisfaction to be gained from driving either of two automobiles.

Illustrations can also support an effective paragraph of comparison. Since an illustration can be presented to the reader in the form of a single narrative account or a series of short accounts, the writer's problem here is to keep in mind that each illustration, long or short, will function as a unit. Both units must have in common a basic similarity and must directly support the controlling idea of the comparison. For example, you might compare the shopping procedures of two economy-minded shoppers. Their *procedures* would be the basis of the comparison and their *thrift* would be the central focus of your total discussion. One smart shopper might go through the advertisements in his or her newspaper looking for items that are on sale. Having determined the best prices, the shopper would then go directly to the stores offering the best prices. Another smart shopper might go to several stores comparing prices of items on display. The first procedure might be used to shop for groceries; the second procedure might be used to shop for an appliance. Either way, thrift is the objective and both procedures will accomplish it. On the other hand, you might want to illustrate the *heroism* (specific quality) of *people in different parts of the world throughout history* (basis of comparison), not as a single illustration but as a series of short actions.

Comparison may be made by means of reasons—your own or someone else's, or both. The basis of the comparison might involve two countries, say China and Greece in their early days, and your controlling idea might be the cultural education encouraged in those civilizations. For example, you might write the following topic sentence and supply reasons similar to those given just below.

TOPIC SENTENCE: Traditional Chinese education was, in some respects, similar to that of Athens in its best days.

1. Athenian boys learned Homer's *Iliad* and *Odyssey* by heart; Chinese boys learned the Confucian classics just as thoroughly.

2. Athenians learned a due respect for their gods which was expressed in outward observance. The Chinese were taught to perform certain rites with respect to ancestor worship.

3. Both the Athenians and the Chinese were eager to enjoy life, and their conception of pleasure was refined by a deep sense of the beautiful.

A paragraph of comparison frequently requires your opinion, judgment, or critical evaluation. You might use reason to show why you prefer one candidate of several running for the same office. Your basis for comparison could be the similar training of, let's say, two of them, the similar personal qualities, conduct in former offices, and the like. Your particular stress might be the greater potential for success in this particular office at this time of the one who is your preference; or, if you have no preference, your focus might be on the adequate qualifications of both candidates for the office, with the final choice left to the voters.

You are likely to be called upon to write paragraphs of comparison in many of your classes or in the course of your occupation. For instance, a history question might be, "In what ways did the Battle of Concord resemble the Battle of Bull Run?" Or, "What features did the Age of Pericles in Greece and the Age of Augustus in Rome have in common?" In your work you might be asked to compare two similar products made by different manufacturers or to compare two courses of action. Comparison can be a very effective method of convincing people. Notice how frequently it is used in advertising where "Brand X" is compared with the product being advertised.

In such assignments your paragraph should be a well-developed piece of comparison. You must show only those matters that are similar. You must have a basis of comparison and a specific quality, point, or issue toward which to work and to control what you say and how you say it. You must also keep in mind that your basic materials (detail, reason, and illustration) should be arranged in an appropriate order (time order, general-to-specific, climactic importance, or other) so that the coherence of the paragraph will be maintained as effectively as possible. And finally, you must remember that comparison has to do only with similarities of the things being compared and that the whole paragraph should be composed from that point of view.

Here are several paragraphs of comparison, each developed primarily by a different basic material. The first one, using detail in general-to-specific order, compares a dog and his master, both of them disreputable characters. The writer—a student—is composing the paragraph as if from the point of view of an uneducated person, although certainly an observant one.

They were inseparable—Old Man Mooney and his dog—and alike as two peas popped from the same pod. They had big, rheumy eyes— both of them. You know—that pale, faded, watery kind of blue that makes you want to look somewhere else in a hurry. Then like that wasn't enough, those eyes were sunk in dark, deep sockets. Old Man Mooney near to scared the life out of people that didn't know him with them eyes—and even the bravest of us weren't hankerin' to meet up with that mongrel of his in the dead of night. They were a spindly-shanked, wobbly pair, and both of 'em lean, hard, and dirty. The old man was bearded, and his hair straggly, hangin' over his ears. And the dog was always a mess—his dirty, mangy coat hangin' in tufted wisps and patches over his lean, scabby body. And friendly—those two were about as friendly as a mother wildcat with a brood of new-born kittens. They were a perfectly matched set of the meanest and ugliest dispositions you'd ever find. That old cur—he had a big, mean, smashed-up face, with a wicked-lookin' mouth and jowls hangin' down around his knees. And Old Mooney's face—maybe it didn't quite come to hangin' down around his knees, but I ain't seen a longer or meaner one in many a year. They even behaved the same way. People knew 'em both for how miserly they were. The old man hoarded every penny, every scrap of paper, every bit of string he found. And that ugly cur—him too—hoardin' every bit of bone, every filthy stick he found. Old Man Mooney and his dog—yessirree!— ain't never seen such likeness and hope never to again. They're both dead now. [54]

DIANE GROSSETT   [A student]

The next paragraph shows that no one nation or people has a monopoly on courageous acts. Drawing upon material generally familiar to most readers, the writer arranges in pairs comparable heroic actions, each belonging to a different country, writes them as illustrations to prove the validity of the controlling idea, and finally organizes the three sets of heroic deeds in time order. (There are two things to notice in this paragraph. First, the illustrations within each set are also in time order. Second, this one long paragraph could be divided into three short paragraphs, each with its own topic sentence.)

The history of the Western world is notable for acts of heroism by men who sought only to perform their duty. Early records tell of two noblemen who gave their lives in defense of their country and their king. In ancient Greece, a handful of men, both Athenian and Spartan, under Leonidas held the narrow pass of Thermopylae against the surging hordes of Persians in an attempt to save Athens and the Greek peninsula. Centuries later in the Pyrenees, Count Roland and a small band of French soldiers died in the pass of Roncesvalles fighting a rear-guard action against Basque mountaineers to protect the main body of Charlemagne's army. Sometimes heroic deeds are the result of error or misjudgment. In 1854 at Balaklava in the Crimea an English cavalry brigade, ordered to retake guns lost to the enemy, charged into the face of Russian artillery and lost two-thirds of its men because someone had blundered. Then, some twenty years later in southern Montana, General Custer and his men of the Seventh Cavalry, owing to a tactical misjudgment bravely fought against Chief Crazy Horse at the Little Big Horn and were annihilated. In recent times both professional soldiers and civilians have performed deeds of valor on the front lines of battle. During World War II at the evacuation of Dunkerque every available nonmilitary boat, manned by civilians, crossed the Channel to rescue thousands of British and French soldiers caught in a squeeze when France fell to the Germans. Two years later, the Russians at Stalingrad endured for months the heavy bombing by the German army, fought a guerilla war during the fall and winter, and, finally, after untold hardship and tremendous casualties, mounted a counteroffensive that defeated the enemy and perhaps turned the direction of the war in favor of the Allies.

In the following paragraph the writer uses unchanging human nature as his basis of comparison for primitive and modern man, and as his specific interest the *primitive magic* that has remained in human nature since the beginning of time. The paragraph then specifies how some of the cherished mementos of primitive times and of today seem to express that magic. In the primitive mentality a thing that had been in contact with a living person became magically imbued with some quality or characteristic of that personality, and the primitive person cherished that "thing" for its magic property. Thus today, reasons the writer, we are in some ways like the primitives.

Primitive magic survives in the subconscious. The strand of hair is carried in the locket, grandmother's wedding dress, the faded fan of the first ball, the regimental badge, all have a half-conscious fetish character. The bobby-soxers who tear shreds off the crooner's garb are the vulgarized twentieth-century version of the worshippers cherishing a splinter from a saint's bone. The value that we set on original manuscripts, on "signed" pieces of furniture, on Dickens' quill and Kepler's telescope, are more dignified manifestations of the same unconscious tendency. It is, as the child said, "jolly nice" to behold a fragment of a marble by Praxiteles—even if it is battered out of human shape, with a leper's nose and broken ears. The contact with the master's hand has imbued it with a magic quality which has lingered on and radiates at us, conveying the same thrill as "the real blood on Nelson's real shirt." [55]

ARTHUR KOESTLER   "The Anatomy of Snobbery"

In a paragraph of comparison you have a slightly more difficult problem in arranging your sentences than in the simple type of development with which you are now familiar. In addition to the basic orders for coherence, discussed in Chapter 4, you should also decide whether to express the comparison in one sentence. Consider the example below:

TOPIC SENTENCE: Primitive magic survives in the subconscious.

> The headhunter carried the shriveled head of an enemy strapped to his belt; the modern puts strands of hair in a locket that she wears about her neck.

In the alternative, the parts of the comparison would be expressed in a succession of sentences.

> The headhunter carried the shriveled head of an enemy strapped to his belt. The modern puts strands of hair in a locket that she wears about her neck.

Still again, you might say everything you plan to say about the primitive before you say anything about the modern. For example:

> The headhunter carried the shriveled head of an enemy strapped to his belt. The early Christian treasured a splinter from a saint's bone. The worshiper of Greek art gloried in a fragment from a marble by Praxiteles. Similarly, the modern puts strands of hair in a locket that she wears about her neck. The bobby-soxers tear shreds off the crooner's garb. The hero-worshiper gets a thrill from seeing the real blood on Nelson's real shirt.

The form you choose for your paragraphs of comparison will be determined by the nature of your materials, your own preferences, and what you consider to be the most effective for the reader.

Before we leave our discussion of comparison, you should know that analogy, which is an extended comparison, is often used in full paragraph form to explain a complex subject or for more artistic effect. As a type of paragraph development, therefore, analogy will be discussed later in this chapter.

¶ Exercises

A. Despite the American prohibition on "comparing apples with oranges," write a short paragraph in which you do just that.

B. Write a paragraph in which you compare two compact automobiles, one of American and one of Japanese manufacture. Do not express a preference for either.

C. Rewrite the paragraph called for in B above in which you *do* show your preference.

Contrast

The purpose of contrast is to show the *difference* between two persons, places, things, or ideas. Two brothers may resemble each other in various ways, but they may also be very unlike in appearance or personality. One may be tall, the other short; one may be generous, the other selfish. Although New York and San Francisco are both port cities, one may be progressive, the other backward. While both *free* and *independent* refer to general freedom from restraint, there are particular differences that any good dictionary will make clear. In a paragraph of contrast, therefore, only those materials that show the differences, the *dissimilarities,* should be included.

In addition, the paragraph of contrast needs a basis of contrast and a specific dominant quality, point, or issue, probably the controlling idea, to give the necessary unity. In the preceding examples, the brothers are both *boys,* New York and San Francisco are both *port cities,* and *free* and *independent* are both qualities. Thus in each case the two things being contrasted are in the same class and therefore may be contrasted. However, until some central focus is provided that will give a unifying purpose to the details, reasons, or illustrations chosen as basic material, the paragraph as an artistic piece of composition cannot succeed.

Let us repeat here the procedure used in analyzing the Byron-Hemingway paragraph in the section on comparison; but this time we shall apply it to material in a paragraph of contrast. In the paragraph below the writer is contrasting several characteristics of the ancient Greeks and the Chinese. For his basis of contrast he uses the material temperaments of each people; as his specific interest he chooses the contrasting qualities of "energetic" and "indo-lcnt." His paragraph of contrast will, therefore, attempt to show that these ancient, cultured peoples were different in their basic temperaments, especially with respect to energy and indolence. For supporting materials he uses reason and illustration.

> The great difference between the temperaments of the ancient Greeks and Chinese was that the Greeks were energetic and the Chinese were indolent. [1]The Greeks turned their ardors toward art and science and the destruction of each other. [2]The Chinese indolence inclined to poetry and meditation and the observance of a golden rule as expressed by Confucius. [3]Politics attracted the passions of the Greeks. [4]Even when one of them was forced from office, he might head a group of "patriots" and attack his native city. [5]Political office for the Chinese was a necessity to which he submitted and indifferently served out an unfortunate tenure. [6]When a Chinese official was disgraced or let out, he returned happily to his native province and wrote poetry about the joys of country life. [7]In time the Greek civilization destroyed itself, but the Chinese had to be destroyed, if at all, by forces from outside its borders.

As before, we can list the major and minor supporting statements, which are numbered.

1. *Major:* The Greeks turned to art, science, and self-destruction.
2. *Major:* The Chinese inclined to poetry, meditation, and a golden rule.
3. *Major:* The Greeks were passionately interested in politics.
4. *Minor:* An ousted Greek became belligerent against his own city.
5. *Major:* The Chinese were indifferent to politics.
6. *Minor:* An ousted Chinese went home and wrote poetry.
7. *Major:* The Greek civilization destroyed itself; the Chinese did not.

From this analysis we can see that the major statements directly support the controlling idea: the contrasting temperaments of energy and indolence. The minor statements support the major statements and the controlling idea of the paragraph. Since all materials conform to the basis of contrast and to the central focus predetermined by the writer, the paragraph is unified. The paragraph is also coherent because it follows properly the general-to-specific order chosen at the start.

Detail, illustration, and reason, alone or in combination, may also be used to develop a paragraph of contrast. You might use details to present differences between boys and girls in an educational situation that is helping to perpetuate disparities (or breaking down the differences) between the sexes. Based on sociologists' reports, boys are the maladjusted, the low achievers, the truants, the delinquents, the inattentive, and the rebellious. Findings of contrasting qualities in the girls make them out to be the well-adjusted, the high scholastic achievers, the attentive, and the more submissive to authority.

In a paragraph of contrast you might illustrate one or more of the above qualities. For example, two brothers from the same family might reach completely different ends because one of them submitted to tight parental control and the other asserted independence from such guidance. Or a paragraph might show by anecdotes a difference in the attitude of a school toward its athletic program and its academic curriculum, where both are advocated by the administration as major parts of a student's education.

For a paragraph contrasting the achievements of a five-year period ending this year with any other five-year period in the twentieth century, you could easily use reason. The paragraph would consist of your judgments, your opinions, as to why the present period is more or less notable than the other period. Or you might contrast two candidates for office, each with different training and experience, only one having the potential for success, the deciding factor being a sense of duty or a reputation for reliability.

In a paragraph of contrast, as in one of comparison, you can express the contrasting elements in one sentence, in alternate sentences, or in groupings of several sentences each. Again, your choice will depend upon what seems the more effective presentation.

The method of contrast is often effective in an analytical presentation of characteristics that make up the two sides of a conflict. In the following paragraph the writer contrasts certain characteristics of the negotiating process that may be observed by a political scientist. The basis of contrast is a group of Americans and Soviets facing each other. The main emphasis is the conflict that has long existed, and the basic material to support the controlling idea is detail, arranged in general-to-specific order.

> Once seated but during the few minutes before the formal negotiations at the Summit Conference started, the people on the two sides of the table presented a study in differences. The Soviet negotiators were grim and silent as they studied their papers, heads bowed. None of them looked up, apparently reluctant to show by body language any acknowl-

edgement of their counterparts across the table. Even the chief Soviet negotiator, his back to his counterpart, talked in whispers to the aide behind him. On the other side of the table, the U.S. negotiators carried on animated conversations among themselves, their papers untouched and unopened before them. Finally, as the Soviet faces came up, a line of scowls was met by a line of smiles. Dark pessimism and suspicion met a cheerful optimism and openness. Although not a word had been spoken across the table, the negotiations were underway.

In recent years considerable overemphasis has been placed on athletics in the total educational program. Concerning this issue the writer of the next paragraph, having considered several sports, concludes that the real difference among them is the part played by the spectator. The paragraph gives his reasons for his conclusion. Furthermore, the paragraph is arranged in mildly climactic order developed in two parts: in the first half, where he names individual sports, one senses that there is a decreasing need by the players of spectator participation; in the second half, there is increasing need.

Unlike any other sport, football is played solely for the benefit of the spectator. If you take the spectator away from any other game, the game could survive on its own. Thus tennis players love tennis, whether or not anyone is watching. Golfers are almost churlish in their dedication to their game. Ping-pong players never look around. Basketball players can dribble and shoot for hours without hearing a single cheer. Even baseball might survive the deprivation, despite the lack of parks. Softball surely would. But if you take away the spectators, if you demolished the grandstands and boarded up the stadium, it is inconceivable to think that any football would be played in the eerie privacy of the field itself. No football team ever plays another team just for the fun of playing football. Army plays Navy, Michigan plays Purdue, P.S. 123 plays P.S. 124, only with the prospect of a loud crowd on hand. [56]

WADE THOMPSON   "My Crusade Against Football"

¶ Exercises

A. Read the following passage carefully and then evaluate it as a paragraph of contrast by answering the questions that appear below it.

[1]When Flora Belle and Daisy Pied set out to landscape their two 50-by-70-foot back yards, they must have vowed most determinedly to make their gardens as different as two gardens could possibly be. [2]In the left rear corner of her lot Flora planted a Norwegian spruce; Daisy set out rambler roses on a trellis the neighbor boy put together. [3]In her right corner Flora put in peonies; Daisy had a Chinese elm. [4]Bordering three sides of her yard Daisy planted a privet hedge, the prickly kind. [5]Flora erected one of those Virginia fences with top and bottom rails and cross pieces between. [6]Up the center of the lawn, from hedge to house, Daisy had the mason build a stone walk; Flora figured walking on the grass was what grass was intended for. [7]Flora's final bit of landscaping was a summer sitting platform with roof and latticed sides for the morning glories to climb over. [8]Daisy hung a hammock she could rest her body in. [9]By the way, that vow they must have taken back at the start of their fixing up was a thunderin' success. [10]Neither one has spoken to the other in five years come this fall.

1. What is the basis for contrast?
2. What is the specific dominant quality, point, or issue?
3. Is the controlling idea satisfactory?
4. Is the paragraph unified?
5. What type of basic material is used?
6. What is the order of development?
7. Which sentences, if any, do not belong in the paragraph?
8. What does their presence or absence tell you about the effectiveness of this paragraph?

B. Write a paragraph contrasting one of the following pairs:

- The methods of two different teachers
- A supermarket and a corner grocery store
- Air travel and automobile travel
- Day and night
- Television and radio

Combined Comparison and Contrast

Occasionally, because you wish to achieve a close relationship between two constituent parts of a subject, you may decide to combine comparison and contrast in the same paragraph. If so, you can follow the procedures, suggested earlier, of putting the compared (or contrasted) materials in a single sentence, in alternate sentences, or in groupings of several sentences. Should you use the last of these methods, be sure to insert between the groupings, for the sake of good coherence, some word, phrase, or sentence that shows you are making a transition from the one to the other.

The writer of the following paragraph, combining comparison and contrast, wished to show the similarities and the dissimilarities between Pompey and Caesar in their bid for fame. He decided to present the comparisons first, and then the contrasts. Following his topic sentence ("Swept along on a tide of achievements, both Pompey and Julius Caesar rose to fame in the eyes of the Roman populace, but when Pompey sought to seize the crown of laurel from the more capable Caesar, destiny stepped in."), the writer then expressed the comparative details in the first part of the paragraph and the contrasting material in the last portion. The rest of the paragraph follows:

[1]Both Pompey and Julius Caesar were first-rate generals supported by personal armies of professional soldiers, and both became contemptuous of the Senate that tried to curb them. [2]The egotistical Pompey began his career with brilliant conquests of Spain and the eastern kingdoms of Alexander, while the no less dashing Caesar thrilled the Roman populace with his nine-year conquest of Gaul. [3]Both realized that the republic had outlived its usefulness, but each wanted to be a dictator. [4]At first they worked together (with Crassus) in the First Triumvirate (60 B.C.) to force reforms upon the unwilling Senate. [5]But eventually Pompey took advantage of Caesar's absence in Gaul to become sole dictator in Rome, whereupon Caesar with one of his legions crossed the Rubicon River, part of the northern boundary of Italy (the occasion for his famous "The die is cast") and accumulated a personal army for his march on Rome. [6]In the battles that followed, Pompey showed bad judgment and irresolution and was destroyed by the superior generalship of Caesar at Pharsalia (48 B.C.). [57]

ROBERT WARNOCK and GEORGE K. ANDERSON   *The Ancient Foundations*

Here the writer unifies his discussion around the basis of comparison and of contrast—the *two Roman generals*—and the central focus of their *bid for fame.* He shows that their lives at first moved along parallel lines, and then diverged. Structurally, the turn comes when Pompey took advantage of Caesar. Before that moment their interests and actions were similar, and the first part of the paragraph is comparison; after that moment their interests and activities were dissimilar, and the rest of the paragraph is contrast. Before the turn, both men were successful; afterward, one went down in defeat, the other rose to power.

This paragraph is also notable for its use in only six sentences of all the basic materials of paragraph development: detail, illustration, and reason. Sentence 1 compares the two men by means of detail; sentence 2 uses illustrations; sentence 3, reason; sentence 4, illustration; sentence 5, illustration; and sentence 6, reason. Moreover, the transition from comparison to contrast is marked by the words, "But eventually."

Biographers have not agreed on the true character of George Washington. Many depict him as a serene old man; others, as a man possessing youthful passions and ambitions throughout his life. Samuel Eliot Morison in the next paragraph, seeking to balance these impressions, explains that Washington at times did conform to the serene "old age" image, but that he also showed throughout his life many youthful qualities not usually associated with the "Father of his Country." Thus the writer uses comparison to show that Washington's character was partly like the general impression, and uses contrast to reveal that it was partly quite the opposite. The basic material of the paragraph is primarily the citation of reasons, with one or two sentences of illustration.

> Perhaps it is not the fault of the painters and biographers that we think of Washington as an old man, but because his outstanding qualities—wisdom, poise, and serenity—are not the qualities usually associated with youth. He seemed to have absorbed, wrote Emerson, "all the serenity of America, and left none for his restless, rickety, hysterical countrymen." The Comte de Chastellux, one of the French officers in the war, said that Washington's most characteristic feature was balance: "the perfect harmony existing between the physical and moral attributes of which he is made up." Yet Gilbert Stuart, after painting his first portrait of Washington, said that "all his features were indicative of the most ungovernable passions, and had he been born in the forests," it was

his opinion that "he would have been the fiercest man among the savage tribes." Both men were right. Washington's qualities were so balanced that his talents, which were great but nothing extraordinary, were more effective in the long run than those of greater generals like Napoleon, or of bolder and more original statesmen like Hamilton and Jefferson. Yet as a young man Washington was impatient and passionate, eager for glory in war, wealth in land, and success in love. Even in maturity his fierce temper would sometimes get the better of him. Here in Cambridge, at his headquarters in the Craigie House, he once become so exasperated at the squabbling of drunken soldiers in the front yard that, forgetting the dignity of a general, he rushed forth and "laid out" a few of the brawlers with his own fists; and then much relieved, returned to his study. Under great provocation he would break out with a torrent of Olympian oaths that terrified the younger men on his staff. Tobias Lear, the smooth young Harvard graduate who became Washington's private secretary, admitted that the most dreadful experience in his life was hearing the General swear.[58]

SAMUEL ELIOT MORISON   *The Young Man Washington*

One more example. The following paragraph begins with a comparison between two marks of punctuation, and then develops a basis for contrast between them. Notice the comparison the writer makes in the last sentence of the paragraph. This is a good example of an analogy, a device discussed in the last section of this chapter.

The two forms of punctuation which are constantly used for aesthetic, often dramatic, purposes are the semicolon and the question mark. The semicolon is our most dignified mark of punctuation. As the question mark calls for excitement and involvement, so the semicolon demands silence and reflection. It means far more than merely a long pause for which a comma is insufficient. It is perhaps rather like a bridge across some quiet stream—a bridge upon which one stands to survey silently what has gone before and to prepare oneself for what is to come.[59]

MARY ELLEN CHASE   "Why Teach Literature?"

When you use comparison or contrast to develop a paragraph, be guided by the following rules:

1. *Comparison needs a basis of comparison; contrast needs a basis of contrast.*
2. *Both need a specific dominant quality, point, or issue (controlling idea) by which you will be governed in the selection of basic materials.*
3. *Comparison deals only with similarities.*
4. *Contrast deals only with dissimilarities.*
5. *Both require that materials be placed in some predetermined order for good coherence.*

¶ Exercise

Write a single paragraph developed by both comparison and contrast in which you weigh certain features and reach a decision or conclusion regarding

1. Different means of transportation from one place to another
2. Two different places to go for a vacation
3. Two different brands of products used for the same purpose
4. An apple and an orange
5. Badminton and tennis
6. A waterbed and a regular bed

You must be very careful to limit your topic sentence in order to prepare the reader for the double task of comparison and contrast in the same paragraph. And remember that your paragraph could well be longer than one of *either* comparison or contrast.

Analogy

An analogy is a detailed comparison. Used properly, analogy can be a powerful means by which the writer may make a point. Analogy is, in essence, a logic *system* which depends on an assumption that if A and B have certain known similarities, they could also have further similarities. Be warned, however, that the making of assumptions can be dangerous. One of the uses of analogy, then, is a way of reasoning. The value of analogy is that it can lead to insights or hunches that in turn lead to important discoveries.

First let us look at an analogy that *could* be invalid:

City *A* has parks, attractive residential areas, a university, and good public spirit. City *B* has parks, attractive residential areas, and a university. Therefore, you are asked to believe that City *B* has good public spirit. The trouble with this analogy is that there are just too many variables that are not included in it. There could well be a poor relationship between the people at the university and the people in the town. There might be an unpleasant political climate in City *B* which limits progress or development there. In other words, parks, attractive residential areas, and a university do not necessarily mean that public spirit is good in a given city.

The use of analogy as it relates to paragraph writing is a way of explaining something. In this kind of analogy, the unfamiliar thing is explained in terms of a familiar one that is similar in certain respects. You use this kind of analogy when you demonstrate the rotation of the earth to a child by means of a ball or top. You might also describe the geographic shape of Italy as similar to the shape of a boot. This kind of analogy depends upon the *resemblance,* not the *actual likeness,* between the things compared.

Such analogies occur most frequently in single sentences. For example:

- The *clergyman* serves the *parish* as the *shepherd* serves the *flock.*
- A *mayor* governs a *city* much as a *captain* commands a *ship.*
- A *navigator* describes the position of his or her vessel in terms of *degrees east or west of the meridian that passes through Greenwich, England, and degrees north or south of the equator;* a *resident* describes the location of his or her house by the *name of the street and its number on it.*

In the last analogy above, either of the two parts of it could be analogized to the plotting of a point on a graph in terms of the horizontal axis and the vertical axis.

But when there are a number of points of resemblance, the explanation can be expanded point by point throughout the paragraph.

Analogy of this type is often used in scientific explanations when the writer seeks to make clear a little-known subject by comparing it with a subject clearly understood. For example, in discussing the effect of the sun on chlorophyll molecules, the author of the next paragraph compares the particles of sunlight to bullets from a machine gun.

Light, in the latest theory, is not waves in a sea of ether, or a jet from a nozzle; it could be compared rather to machine gun fire, every photo-electric bullet of energy traveling in regular rhythm, at a speed that bridges the astronomical gap in eight minutes. As each bullet hits an electron of chlorophyll, it sets it to vibrating, at its own rate, just as one tuning fork, when struck, will cause another to hum in the same pitch. A bullet strikes—and one electron is knocked galley west into a dervish dance like the madness of the atoms in the sun. The energy splits open chlorophyll molecules, recombines their atoms, and lies there, dormant, in foods. [60]

DONALD CULROSS PEATTIE   "Chlorophyll: The Sun Trap"

As you can see, this analogy compares two things—the sun's particles and machine-gun bullets—but the things are not in the same class. However, the relation between the sun and its particles of light is like the relation between the machine gun and bullets. The sun's particles hit the molecules of chlorophyll and break them apart; the gun's bullets hit an object and shatter it. Thus the relation between the action of the sun and the action of the gun, between the particles of light striking the molecules and the bullets shattering an object, is similar. In all other respects, the sun and the gun, the particles and the bullets, are different. However, in that one resemblance lies the basis of the analogy.

In discussing comparison and contrast, we said that a paragraph should have not only a basis of comparison or contrast, but also a central focus, the controlling idea, that establishes and maintains the dominant quality, impression, or issue being presented. The paragraph of analogy likewise needs both a basis of analogy and a central focus since it is an extended type of comparison. We have just seen how in the making of chlorophyll the sun and the machine gun, though in different classes, bear a resemblance that serves as the basis of analogy. The *central focus* would be the process of the sun that provides the chlorophyll for plants.

As long as you keep the basis of analogy in mind and adapt your materials to the central focus of the paragraph, permitting nothing to intrude that is irrelevant to your main purpose, your paragraph will be properly unified. Then, if you are careful to arrange materials in a predetermined order that keeps the idea of the paragraph flowing smoothly and in accordance with the analogy itself, the paragraph will be coherent. Moreover, if you are interested in attempting to be creative, the paragraph of analogy may be fun to write.

Most of us depend upon analogy more often than we realize. In the following paragraph the author names parts of the body, one by one, and suggests an analogous relationship with some part of another object. She uses detail as the basic material, analogy as the method of development, and arranges her analogies in general-to-specific order.

> Parts of the body are further used in reference to many things which are themselves concrete and familiar. We speak of the "lip" and "ears" of a cup, the "teeth" of a saw or comb, the "legs" of tables and the other immobile articles of furniture, the "elbows" of pipes and macaroni, the "hands" of a clock, the "tongue" of a balance or a bell, the "eye" of a needle, and the "head" of a hammer. When we travel, we encounter the "foot" of a mountain, the "mouth" of a river, a "head"-land, the "shoulders"—even the "soft shoulders"—of a road, the "brow" of a hill, and the "neck" of the woods. The German speaks eloquently of a *Meeresbusen* ("bosom" of the sea or gulf). Slightly disguised from us today [is] the "core" (heart) of an apple—a Romance word. . . . In politics we hear of a "rump" parliament and a "head" of state. Perhaps "ward-heeler" may be included here, though it is actually a compound. [61]
>
> MARGARET SCHLAUCH   *A Gift of Tongues*

In the next paragraph, the writer constructs an elaborate analogy that illuminates an important difference between written and spoken forms of language. The paragraph uses reasons arranged in climactic order.

> The ice borrows its substance from the river, it is indeed the actual water of the river itself—and yet it is not the river. A child, seeing the ice, thinks that the river exists no more, that its course has been arrested. But this is only an illusion. Under the layer of ice, the river continues to flow down to the plain. Should the ice break, one sees the water suddenly bubble up as it goes gushing and murmuring on its way. This is an image of the stream of language. The written tongue is the film of ice upon its waters; the stream which still flows under the ice that imprisons it is the popular and natural language; the cold which produces the ice and would fain restrain the flood is the stabilizing action exerted by grammarians and pedagogues; and the sunbeam which gives lan-

guage its liberty is the indomitable force of life, triumphing over rules and breaking the fetters of tradition. [62]

JOSEPH VENDRYES *Language: A Linguistic Introduction to History*

History provides a natural source of analogies, since the events or situations of one time may resemble those of another time. One of the most famous literary analogies was created by Victor Hugo when he described the battlefield of Waterloo. It uses detail as its basic materials, arranged in space order.

Those who wish to form a clear idea of the battle of Waterloo need only imagine a capital *A* laid on the ground. The left stroke of the *A* is the Nivelles road, the right one the Genappe road, while the cross of the *A* is the sunken road from Ohain to Braine l'Alleud. The top of the *A* is Mont-Saint-Jean; Wellington is there; the left-hand lower point is Hougomont; Reille is there with Jerome Bonaparte. The right-hand lower point is La Belle Alliance; Napoleon is there. A little below where the cross of the *A* meets the right stroke is La Haye Sainte; in the center of this cross is the precise point where the final battle-word was spoken. It is here that the lion is placed, the involuntary symbol of the supreme heroism of the Imperial Guard. The triangle contained at the top of the *A* between the two strokes of the cross is the plateau of Mont-Saint-Jean. The dispute for this plateau was the whole battle. [63]

Les Miserables

Here, finally, are two paragraphs of analogy that cleverly set in opposition a man's experiences with automobiles. The author begins his article, from which the selections are taken: "Once upon a time, the American met the automobile and fell in love. Unfortunately, this led him into matrimony, and so he did not live happily ever after." With matrimony as the central focus, the first paragraph depicts the man enduring the caprices of a fretful wife; the second shows the "husband" shifting his interests when the "nagging wife" has done her worst.

Quickly the automobile became the nagging wife, demanding rubbings and shinings and gifts. She put eyebrows over her windshield in the 1920's, plucked them out in the late 1930's, put them on again in the middle 1940's, and took them off once more in the 1950's. She nagged him for bits of chrome and cursed him for his extravagance when he brought them home. She lifted her face—expensively—from year to year; incessantly demanded new gauds and different colors, developed even more costly eating habits, threatened to break the family budget and often succeeded, and the American—poor dolt—not only catered to her whims but decked her out in dooredge guards and silvery Kleenex dispensers. . . .

In view of these metamorphoses, it is understandable that the American began to stray. In the mid-1950's, he eyed the European car, and found her good. She was petite, she was new, she was gay, she was inexpensive, she bumped and she ground, and like all mistresses, she promised prestige. Maintaining a mistress when one is married to a Harpy is, however, an intolerable situation, and so we can say that the American's marriage to the American automobile is now at an end, and it is only a matter of minutes to the final pistol shot, although who pulls the trigger has yet to be determined. [64]

JOHN KEATS   *The Insolent Chariots*

¶ Exercises

A. Evaluate the following paragraph of analogy. Be prepared to explain why analogy as used in this paragraph is so effective.

[1]The Bay of Monterey has been compared by no less a person than General Sherman to a bent fishinghook; and the comparison, if less important than the march through Georgia, still shows the eye of a soldier for topography. [2]Santa Cruz sits exposed at the shank; the mouth of the Salinas River is at the middle of the bend; and Monterey itself is cosily ensconced beside the barb. [3]Thus the ancient capital of California faces across the bay, while the Pacific Ocean, though hidden by low hills and forests, bombards her left flank and rear with never-dying surf. [4]In front of the town, the long line of sea beach trends north and north-west, and then westward to enclose the bay. [65]

ROBERT LOUIS STEVENSON   "The Old Pacific Capital"

B. Select some geographic feature—a continent, a cape, a lake, or the like— that resembles some familiar object in shape. Develop the analogy in a paragraph.

C. Write a paragraph using analogy to explain some natural phenomenon, such as the action of the tides, a solar eclipse, or the jet stream. Keep in mind the limitation of your subject in your topic sentence.

7. Planning and Writing a Short Paper

By now you should be fairly comfortable with the process of writing a unified and coherent paragraph. Once you have learned how, it is a relatively simple matter to put paragraphs together in a longer piece of writing. This chapter, therefore, is concerned with the techniques for doing so.

For many years now, schools, colleges, and universities have used the theme as a vehicle for teaching writing. The "weekly theme" continues to be a fairly common requirement because a paragraph, standing alone, is rarely an adequate form of writing. For simplicity sake, we will be using the term "themes" frequently in this chapter. But for that term you could easily substitute the following: letters, memoranda, answers to essay questions in examinations, reports, studies, opinions, analyses, and many more. The point is that the *principles* involved in writing a good theme are applicable to many other types of writing.

We cannot overemphasize the importance of being able to write a good theme! A good letter of application may result in your employment or acceptance in the academic program of your choice. Long hours of study for a history exam will be fruitful only if you can coherently present your material in the answer to an essay question. We would also add parenthetically, however, that the ability to write a good answer depends on your grasp of your material.

Writing a good theme is a matter of procedure; that is, it involves proceeding step-by-step from an idea to a finished product. The steps that we will be examining in detail are listed below:

1. Choosing a topic
2. Writing a thesis sentence

3. Gathering information

4. Organizing materials

5. Developing an outline

6. Writing the first draft

7. Writing an introduction and conclusion

8. Providing transition between paragraphs

9. Revising the first draft

At the end of this chapter, you will find three examples of themes: one on Robin Hood, one on pollution, and one on the income of William Shakespeare. As we examine each of the steps enumerated above, we will lead you step-by-step through the process that resulted in the Robin Hood theme. The theme on pollution is shorter and less complex than the one on Robin Hood. After each theme comes an analysis of the sentences constituting it. The final example, a theme about William Shakespeare's income (and his taxes!) is written in a very informal style that is fitting for the subject matter. You may wish to analyze the sentences in it.

The main differences between a paragraph and a theme are that

A PARAGRAPH HAS	A THEME HAS
A topic sentence	A thesis sentence
A controlling idea	A thesis idea
Every sentence a support of the topic sentence and controlling idea	Every paragraph a support of the thesis sentence and thesis idea
Details, reasons, and illustrations as its basic materials	Paragraphs of details, reasons, and illustrations as its basic materials
Sentences composed and arranged in a plan of major and minor supports	Paragraphs composed and arranged in a plan of major and minor supports
Sentences linked together with appropriate means of coherence	Paragraphs arranged and linked together with appropriate means of coherence

There is not a great deal of difference between a *topic sentence* and a *thesis sentence,* or between a *controlling idea* and a *thesis idea.* The purpose is the same. Both the topic sentence and the thesis sentence are to state for the reader what is to come. Both the controlling idea and the thesis idea are useful to the writer in limiting material to that which is relevant. The *difference* is a matter of breadth. Thus the topic sentence, which will be supported only by several sentences, must be narrow—that is, very limited. The thesis sentence is less narrow or restrictive because it will be supported by many sentences, although these supporting sentences are grouped together in more than one paragraph.

Choosing a Topic

Do not be confused by the heading of this section. "Topic" is not used in the same sense as in the phrase "topic sentence." It is really a matter of what you want to write about. In selecting a topic, unless one is assigned, you should keep two important rules in mind. First, your topic should be one that interests you. Second, it should be limited to what can be covered in a short theme. As you cast about for a topic, you are likely to come up first with some broad general one like these:

- The Middle Ages
- The Cost of Energy
- Women's [or Men's] Athletics
- Computers

A moment's reflection will tell you that whole books have been devoted to each of these subjects and that they cannot be adequately dealt with in a short theme. This does not mean that you must scrap these subjects and look for smaller ones. Instead you might divide them up and write about one of the pieces. For example, "computers" might be logically divided into mainframes, microcomputers, and minicomputers. Still, each of these divisions is probably too broad for a short theme. You might end up with "The Programming Languages That Microcomputers Will Support," or "Mainframe Computers Are Much Faster Than the Smaller Ones."

As another example, let us suppose that "The Middle Ages" is the subject that appeals to you. A first step in limiting this broad topic might be to focus on a particular area—"England in the Middle Ages." Next, you could select a particular aspect of medieval life—social life, architecture, science, or some other. Assuming that you choose social life, the next narrowing could focus on political unrest—"The Revolt against the Monied Class." You now remember that the legendary figure Robin Hood lived in this era. Thus, in a few steps, you have narrowed the general subject of "The Middle Ages" to the far more specific topic of "The Legend of Robin Hood." As you gather material and become more knowledgeable about your topic, you may decide to limit it even further.

¶ Exercises

A. Each of the following topics may be too broad to be covered in a short theme. For each one, write one new topic that further limits the area to be covered. For instance, the topic "Famous Cities" could be limited to "Famous Cities of North America."

   1. Energy Consumption
   2. Crime
   3. Automobile Safety
   4. Endangered Species
   5. The Great Outdoors
   6. Gourmet Cooking
   7. Athletics
   8. Physical Fitness
   9. Stress
   10. Constitutional Rights

B. Choose one of the topics from Exercise A above and limit it in several steps until you are satisfied that it is a manageable topic for a short theme. For example: "Famous Cities of North America"—"Famous Canadian Cities"—"Quebec City"—"Good Dining in Quebec City."

Writing the Thesis Sentence

Once you have limited your topic to a manageable size, you will need to compose a working thesis sentence with a definite thesis idea. As we have already noted, the thesis sentence corresponds to the topic sentence of a paragraph; the thesis idea corresponds to the controlling idea of the topic sentence. The first step is to determine what your topic idea will be since it is the idea with which you will need to test the materials eventually to be included in your paper. Although you could defer actually composing your topic sentence at this time, clearly stating your topic idea now is critical.

Let us assume that you wish to limit your subject to Robin Hood, his band, and the events and people associated with them in North Central England during the thirteenth century. You may have to think long and hard to discover an appropriate thesis idea, or you may come upon one quite simply. "What is there," you ask yourself, "about the Robin Hood legend that interests me and is sufficiently limited in scope, about which I can write a short theme?"

Let's do our thinking together. The topic has to do with a legend. The legend involves the far distant past (the thirteenth century). There is something pleasurable about reliving things in the past. But it is not always easy to identify with people, places, and events in the past—especially a legend.

You, too, may wish you could go back to "the good old days"—to the days of Robin Hood, that delightful character who infuriated the Sheriff of Nottingham by robbing from the rich and giving to the poor. In reality, of course, you cannot go back. But you might experience imaginatively such people, places, and adventures if you had some means of contact to which you personally responded. It might only be a piece of wood from Sherwood Forest, a visit to the grave of Robin Hood, or a guided tour through Robin Hood country. Even some library research might make a vicarious experience possible.

At any rate, begin to fashion on paper a working thesis sentence, keeping in mind the restrictions in word length and subject matter you have set for yourself. Your efforts might read thus:

1. The pleasurable seeking out of Robin Hood and days of Sherwood Forest . . .

2. To relive the days of old requires definite preparation.

3. Reliving former times can be pleasurable.

4. Vicariously reliving the adventures of Robin Hood and his merry band is not

difficult if one has some authority for their having existed and also has source materials as support.

5. Identification with the Robin Hood band is possible if one has knowledge of places they frequented, people they associated with, and events they experienced.

6. If the identification with Robin Hood and his merry band is to seem real and meaningful, one must think of them—at least for the time being and imaginatively—as really having lived, as being something more than just traditional folk heroes.

By now you probably realize that the key to your thesis statement is the idea that identification with Robin Hood and Little John is possible only under certain conditions.

¶ Exercise

Using the topic you limited in the previous exercise or, if you prefer, another of suitable size, write a working thesis sentence for a short theme.

You will be able to write some short themes by drawing wholly on your own knowledge and experience. Others, such as the Robin Hood theme, will send you on a hunt for information. The following brief summary indicates the main sources of information available in most libraries and the kinds of data each is likely to contain. As you become better acquainted with the library you will be using, you will no doubt discover additional resources. Invariably the staff of a library is willing and eager to be helpful to you. So don't hesitate to ask questions!

Summary of Sources of Information

Library Card Catalogue

All of the books, periodicals, and other materials in a library are identified in a file of cards called the *card catalogue*. Each book has at least two cards: an *author card,* filed by the author's last name, and a *title card*. A book of nonfiction also has a card that classifies it according to its subject *(subject card).* A survey of the subject cards gives you the titles of all the books the library has on your subject.

Almanacs

An *almanac* is a yearly compilation of miscellaneous information, some of it relating to the events of the previous year and some of it historical. The wide range of facts to be found in a modern almanac is suggested by this random sampling: amount of U.S. currency in circulation; population of the United States from 1790 to the present; Olympic champions in all events since 1896; passenger traffic at leading airports; winners of Nobel and other major prizes; brief biographies of U.S. presidents. Two major almanacs: *World Almanac and Book of Facts; Information Please Almanac.*

Atlases

An *atlas* is a collection of maps illustrating geographical features of the earth and related information, such as principal crops, population density, annual rainfall, and other climate conditions. Specialized atlases contain maps relating to particular periods of history (the westward movement) or to such special subjects as biblical history or the history of literature.

Some major atlases: *National Geographic Atlas of the World; Rand McNally New Cosmopolitan Atlas; Hammond Medallion World Atlas; Shepard's Historical Atlas.*

Biographical Reference Books

Biographical reference books contain information about well-known people. Some books of this kind include people from all fields of endeavor; others specialize in particular areas.

Some major biographical reference books: *Dictionary of American Biography; Dictionary of National Biography* (British); *Webster's Biographical Dictionary; Current Biography; Twentieth-Century Authors; Who's Who in America; Notable American Women, 1607–1950.*

Encyclopedias

An *encyclopedia* is a book or set of books containing information on all branches of knowledge. Some may be but one volume; others may fill many volumes. The information appears in articles of varying length, alphabetically arranged. Most encyclopedias are kept current with the publication of annual yearbooks; moreover, major encyclopedias are revised frequently to include new information. Encyclopedias usually suggest one or more additional sources of information on major topics.

Some major encyclopedias: *Encyclopaedia Britannica; Encyclopedia Americana; Collier's Encyclopedia; Columbia Encyclopedia.*

The Readers' Guide to Periodical Literature

The *Readers' Guide* is an index to the articles in more than one hundred commonly read magazines. Issues, which appear twice a month, are periodically combined in hard covers for longer periods of time.

Specialized Reference Books

Many specialized reference books are devoted to particular fields. Those listed below are only a sampling. Ask your librarian to recommend specific reference books for the field in which you are working.

- Bartlett's *Familiar Quotations*
- Bullfinch's *Mythology*
- *Encyclopedia of American History*
- Encyclopedia of Social Sciences
- Encyclopedia of World History
- Granger's *Index to Poetry*
- The New Grove Dictionary of Music and Musicians
- McGraw-Hill Encyclopedia of Science
- McGraw-Hill Encyclopedia of World Art
- Webster's New World Dictionary of Business Terms

¶ Exercise

Which library tool or reference book would you consult to find the following items of information? If more than one source is likely to have the information, list the one you would go to first. It may be obvious, but you will probably have to go to a library to complete this exercise.

1. President Jimmy Carter's education
2. Facts about the life of Pete Rose
3. The life of inventor Margaret Knight
4. Books on clairvoyance
5. Information on genetics
6. A definition of the term "bottom line"
7. The symphonies of Sir Edward Elgar
8. The boundaries of European countries in 1939
9. Magazine articles on "supply-side" economics
10. The population of Sturbridge, Massachusetts

Organizing Materials

Whether you get the information for your paper from your present knowledge or from reference books, your next step is the same. You should list all of the ideas you think you can use in your paper. The order in which you list them does not matter at this time. The chief importance is to get your ideas on paper where you can see them and arrange them.

Material for a theme on Robin Hood from which to make a selection appears below:

1. Robin Hood, a medieval hero
2. Listed in thirteenth-century Pipe Roll
3. Robert Hode of Wakefield
4. North Central England and the Robin Hood legend
5. Robin not even possibly historical
6. Robin Hood fictitious
7. A person must be romantic by nature to accept him
8. Location of Robin Hood's grave, then and now, in Yorkshire
9. His gravestone
10. Records regarding Robin Hood at Brighouse, England
11. Piece of oak from Sherwood Forest (personal memento)
12. Popular ballads about Robin Hood

13. "The Gest of Robyn Hood"

14. Little John's grave at Hathersage in Derbyshire

15. Robert Hode of Loxley, near Sheffield

16. Fountains Abbey (or Fountain Dale) and Friar Tuck

17. Robin's adventure with Friar Tuck at Skell River

18. Sheriff of Nottingham versus Robin Hood in city tunnels

19. Present Sheriff of Nottingham

20. Much Robin Hood lore in and about Nottingham

21. Caves under Nottingham Castle and city streets

22. Will Stutely hanging in Nottingham

23. Hathersage and death of Little John

24. Beautiful Derwent River Valley surrounding Hathersage

25. Little John's epitaph

26. His long bow and cuirass

27. Little John's grave opened

28. Maid Marian, Robin Hood's wife

29. In Nottingham's city hall tower: the "Little John" bell

30. Boundaries of Barnsdale Forest: one-sixth size of Sherwood

31. Major Oak in Sherwood Forest

32. Bishop of Hereford robbed by Robin Hood

33. Little John's thigh bone

34. Little John's grave claimed by various places

35. Boundaries of Sherwood Forest

36. Edwinstowe, center of Sherwood

37. Skellbrook-Went River, Askern-Badworth (Barnsdale)

38. Little John and Robin Hood meeting

39. Little John's name

40. Thoresby Hall (near Ollerton in Sherwood Forest)

41. Archery contest in Nottingham to catch Robin Hood

42. Little John winner of archery contest

43. Statues and plaques of Robin and followers in Nottingham

44. At Fountains Abbey: Robin Hood's woods, well, the Skell

45. Kirklees Priory: Robin Hood's death

46. Little John present at Robin's death

47. The Constable robbed by Little John

48. King Richard I's visit to Robin Hood in Sherwood

49. Movies and books about Robin Hood

50. Will Scarlett

51. Robin Hood's locale: Yorkshire, Nottinghamshire, Derbyshire

52. Allan-a-Dale, the minstrel

53. Robin a benefactor of the poor

54. A Robin Hood Well in Barnsdale

55. Protective guards needed by travelers in Barnsdale

56. Authenticity of Robin Hood's grave challenged

57. Robin Hood murdered

Many of your selected items will make up the body or main section of the theme, some the introduction and possibly the conclusion, and others will be deleted.

Certain numbered items by virtue of subject matter will cluster around a common central or controlling idea, and in a list as long as this one there may be at least a half dozen clusters. You should find the core idea of each cluster and the related items. Run your eye down the complete list several times, slowly, allowing topics to fall together in a natural kind of association. Core ideas for the present list may be *persons, places, things, activities, and miscellaneous.* That is, all items, no matter how they are worded, that refer basically to people will cluster around the core idea *persons;* all locations like cities, forests, graveyards will associate with *places,* and so forth. Items that do not fit the first four labels should be put with *miscellaneous.*

Next, determine which core idea with its own cluster of topics can most readily absorb many of the items in the other clusters. That is, can most of the topics associated with the *persons, places,* and *things* labels fit under *activities?* Or would the items in the *persons, things,* and *activities* clusters fit better under *places?* Since persons do things in places (Robin Hood shoots an arrow in Sherwood Forest), it seems reasonable, especially for the present list, that *places* is the core idea that will most readily absorb many items in the other clusters.

Let's illustrate what has just been said. From the original list of topics a choice of all items that belong with the core idea *places* would include 4, 8, 16, 20, 21, 23, 24, 30, 34, 35, 36, 37, 38, 40, 44, 45, 51, 54, and 55. Now, combining items in this group that belong together—for instance, 51 with 4 (the latter item being the more general topic), 21 with 20, 37 with 30, 36 with 35, and 8 with 45—we could have five groups. Add two single-item groups (16 and 23) and we have seven, each with a general topic; namely, 4, 16, 20, 23, 30, 35, and 45. The unassigned topics—15, 24, 34, 40, and 56—should be deleted.

Next, from those topics now remaining in the original list, distribute as many as possible among the seven groups just classified under the *places* label. Be sure to put each selected item in the group with which it is most closely associated by subject matter. The result is seven groups of related topics:

1. North Central England: locale of Robin Hood activity in ballads   4, 13, 51
2. Fountains Abbey and Friar Tuck   16, 17, 44
3. City of Nottingham and Robin Hood   18, 20, 21, 22, 29, 41, 42, 43
4. Hathersage: Death of Little John   14, 23, 25, 26, 27, 33
5. Boundaries of Barnsdale Forest   30, 37, 38, 39, 54, 55
6. Boundaries of Sherwood Forest   28, 31, 32, 35, 36, 47, 48, 50, 52
7. Kirklees Priory: Robin Hood's death   8, 9, 45, 46, 57

Of the unassigned topics, some should be reserved for possible use in the introduction or the conclusion to the theme; the rest can be deleted:

> INTRODUCTION: 1, 5, 6, 11, 53
> CONCLUSION: 7
> DELETION: 3, 10, 19, 49 (Others may be deleted after the following check on your materials and later while making the outline.)

At this point, you are almost ready to compose your final thesis sentence. Before you do, however, you should decide as nearly as you can how many paragraphs your finished theme will have.

Estimating that an average paragraph will be about 150 words long, we can assume that a 500-word theme will have about three paragraphs, with the first sentence of the first paragraph serving the dual function of introduction and thesis sentence. Then the second sentence becomes the topic sentence of the first paragraph. Such a short theme may have no formal conclusion, the final sentence of the last paragraph serving that purpose.

The amount of material already gathered for the Robin Hood theme suggests a longer theme of perhaps 750 words. This longer theme may possibly have a short introduction and conclusion. If introducing and concluding the theme takes about 50 words each, then the body or main portion of the discussion can use approximately 650 words, or about five paragraphs. With a separate introductory paragraph, the *body* begins with the second paragraph of the theme. The first sentence of that paragraph serves as the topic sentence of the body (a unit of several paragraphs similar to a paragraph of several sentences) and has its own controlling idea, which directly supports the thesis idea of the thesis sentence expressed in the introduction. The second sentence of the second paragraph then becomes the topic sentence of that paragraph and directly supports the controlling idea of the body.

Keeping in mind your goal of a 750-word theme in four or five paragraphs (the body accounting for about 650 words), look closely at the seven groups of items that will comprise the body of the theme. The first, North Central England, includes four items that relate to the general background of the whole theme. Instead of making up a single paragraph, these topics, taken separately, would best serve as needed in different parts of the discussion. For instance, items 12 and 13 would be appropriate for the introduction, and 4 and 51 would seem suitable material for the topic sentence and the body. Redistribution of the topics in group 1 leaves only six clusters to be developed.

Group 2, Fountains Abbey and Friar Tuck, should be eliminated. Its three topics (16, 17, and 44) are insufficient for a separate paragraph. Furthermore, two other members of Robin Hood's band—Will Scarlett (item 50) and Allan-a-Dale (item 52)—are merely mentioned in the original list. Most of its topics bear directly or indirectly on Robin Hood and Little John. Therefore, it seems wise to eliminate these two items (50, 52), along with group 2 and reduce the content of the body to only five clusters of topics, that is, sufficient material for five paragraphs.

You are finally ready to compose your thesis sentence. It might be worded like this: *Identifying with Robin Hood and his lieutenant Little John is entirely possible for anyone willing to suppose them real.* Later you may find it desirable to add certain conditions when you write your introduction.

Before you forget it, add the redistributed topic numbers 12 and 13 to the numbers listed for the introduction, and in some way make a note that numbers 4 and 51 may be used in the topic sentence of the body. Double check all the deleted items: 2, 3, 10, 15, 16, 17, 19, 24, 34, 40, 44, 49, 50, and 52.

The Outline

To some, the development of a good working outline is the most difficult part of writing because it takes a great deal of thought. All good writing depends on logical arrangement of the material that you will use. The list of some fifty-seven items we developed for a paper on Robin Hood was a necessary step in the writing process, although there was no particular order or organization to the list. We next did some sorting, putting our items into clusters by topic. Now we must determine the best order and show it in the form of an outline.

Before going on to an actual outline, let us review the conventions of outlining. The main topics should be headed with roman numerals (I, II, and so on); subtopics of them should be headed with upper case (capital) letters (A, B, and so on). Further levels of subtopics in descending order of importance should be headed with Arabic numerals (1, 2, and so on) and finally lower case (small) letters (a, b, and so on). The important thing to remember is that each outline division should be equal in importance to others having the same *type* of numeral or letter. Thus, all those marked with a roman numeral should be of the same importance; so too should those marked with a capital letter.

Topics with the same kind of numeral or letters should be indented to line up vertically as:

```
I.  _____
    A.  _____
        1.  _____
            a.  _____
            b.  _____
        2.  _____
            a.  _____
            b.  _____
    B.  _____
        1.  _____
        2.  _____
II. _____
    A.  _____
    B.  _____
```

Each division in an outline should have at least two parts. If there is an A under a Roman numeral I, there must also be a B. (There may be a C and D also.) Subtopics are *divisions* of the larger topic above them in the outline. Clearly, a topic cannot be divided into fewer than two parts.

Topics and subtopics should begin with a capital letter. No other words should be capitalized, except proper nouns or proper adjectives.

Topics should be words or phrases (not a mixture of both), and not complete sentences.

The terms *Introduction, Body,* and *Conclusion* should not appear in the final outline. They are the organizational units in the writer's mind, not topics to be discussed.

Outlining

Grouping related ideas together is the first step in outlining. Next you will need to arrange the five groups of material in an appropriate order of time, space, general-to-specific, specific-to-general, or climax. Just as you designated greater coherence and effectiveness in the total paragraph by determining which of these orders best served the material, so you should apply one of them to the whole theme. With a map of England beside you (your library will have an atlas with a map of sufficient detail), plot the development of the theme as if you were planning a trip through Robin Hood land. Besides helping you with the order of the major clusters of material, this procedure will help you determine the best order of the topics within the given paragraphs.

The following outline suggests one way of arranging the materials for writing the first draft of the theme.

BACK TO ROBIN HOOD AND LITTLE JOHN

I. City of Nottingham and Robin Hood Lore	4, 20, 51
A. Tunnels and caves as refuge	18, 21
B. Will Stutely hanging	22
C. Archery contest	41, 42
D. Tower bell called "Little John"	29
II. Barnsdale Forest	
A. Size	30
B. Boundaries	37
C. Travelers protected by guards	55
D. Meeting of Robin Hood and Little John	38, 39

Writing the First Draft

With your outline before you and your thesis sentence in mind, you are ready to write your first draft. Whether or not you intend to have an introduction and a conclusion, you should focus your attention on the main body of your composition at this time. Your introduction and conclusion, if you want to include them, will come much more easily once you have written the body of your theme.

Plan to allot one paragraph to each major topic in your outline (those marked by roman numerals). Write your first draft as quickly as possible. You will have time later to make needed improvements; therefore, do not worry at this time about details of punctuation and phrasing.

Introduction and Conclusion

Once you have the body of your theme in first-draft form, you can decide about having an introduction and conclusion. The short theme may not need an introduction as something preliminary to the body of the theme. If it does, the introduction precedes the body, is expressed usually in one paragraph of some fifty words or so, and contains the thesis sentence with its thesis (or controlling) idea. It may have, in addition, a definition of words whose clarity is essential to the reader's understanding of the theme content or the writer's point of view. Its tone should also be in keeping with that of the whole theme: formal or informal, serious or light, objective or personal.

A 500-word theme, however, is more likely to begin with a topic sentence for the *body as a whole, its controlling (or thesis) idea serving to give unity to all the paragraphs of the theme.* The real topic sentence with its controlling idea of that first paragraph then follows immediately, and the paragraph develops as any other. The first sentence of the second paragraph of the theme becomes the topic sentence of that paragraph with its own controlling idea and also relates the paragraph directly to the controlling (or thesis) idea of the topic sentence of the body. In composing the topic sentence of the body of a theme, be very certain that it is worded to cover only what you plan to discuss. Later, when you read the completed paper, be sure that the topic sentence of the body still covers only what you did discuss. The topic or thesis sentence of a body is perhaps the most difficult of all topic sentences to write.

A conclusion may not be necessary in a short theme, especially one of only 500 words. Serving instead can be the final sentence of the last paragraph of the theme, particularly if it seems to close the discussion effectively. At times, the complexity of a subject may suggest a clarifying summary of main points. On the other hand, a writer may choose to point up some conclusion, challenge, or direction to be taken as a result of materials presented in the theme. A conclusion—what to say and when to stop—is not easy to compose, and the old editor's adage about introductions, and especially conclusions, is quite sound: "If in doubt, omit!"

Transitional Expressions

In Chapter 4 you saw the importance of transitional expressions in achieving coherence within a paragraph. Those bridges from one thought to the next are no less important *between* paragraphs. Since each new paragraph represents a new stage in your discussion, an appropriate transition can help your reader follow your train of thought by making clear the relationship between paragraphs.

A smooth transition between paragraphs can be accomplished as simply as by using a pronoun that refers clearly to a person or idea discussed in the preceding paragraph. The pronouns *this, that,* and *these* (and these words used as adjectives) commonly link paragraphs in this way. For example:

> I am out to sell poetry to people who don't read it, who don't like it, who don't want their children to read it, and who, especially, don't want their friends and business associates to think they read it. I want not only to persuade them to read poems but as well to transform them into a band of missionary spirits who, suspending poems on every shining television aerial, will convert the American landscape into a forest leafing out in literature.
>
> I have no illusions, of course, as to the possibilities of my succeeding in *this* project. . . . [italics added] [66]
>
> JOHN UNTERECKER "Poetry for the Perfectly Practical Man"

Most of the transitional words and expressions listed on page 91 can be used to show the relationships between as well as within paragraphs. Of these, *then* is often used to introduce a paragraph that sums up or continues the thought of the preceding one.

> It appears, *then,* that we have two distinctly different vocabularies. . . .

Clearly the paragraph that precedes this sentence must give reasons for thinking that people have two vocabularies, not just one. The paragraph that this sentence introduces will presumably define the differences between the two vocabularies.

Overuse of such transitional expressions as *then, however,* and *on the other hand* produces a mechanical effect. But, appropriately used, such expressions can be a help to the reader in following a change in thought or in perceiving a relationship.

¶ Exercises

Each of the following sentences is the first sentence taken from a paragraph. Identify the transitional device in each that appears intended to link the new paragraph to the one before it.

1. And these things, too, will pass.

2. Still, they were not events for us to speculate on.

3. Despite the length of the journey, however, we did enjoy the day.

4. Such was the situation that confronted us.

5. It was fortunate that we had prepared for rain.

6. And yet there is one important point that we have not mentioned.

7. Of course this left us even more mystified.

8. But our work proved to be in vain.

Revising the First Draft

Once you have written your first draft, it is a good idea to put it aside for a while. There is a good reason for this. Writing and revising are very different processes. Writing is impulsive and associative, that is, it is the creative part. Revising, on the other hand, should be deliberate and analytical. *Your first draft should include most of what you want to say. The purpose of the revision is to improve on the way you want to say it.* It is not always easy to criticize your own work, but surely good writing depends on it. Most of us have had the experience of writing something, putting it aside, and going back to it only to find that it needed a great deal of work. You may find that you are well-pleased with your first draft as you complete it. Two days later, however, you may have second thoughts.

There are several techniques that will help you in the revision process. One, mentioned earlier, is to read aloud your draft. Frequently the ear will pick up awkward phrasing that the eye fails to see. Another useful technique is to pretend that you are the reader and not the writer. By so doing you can question whether or not you have provided sufficient illustrations, reasons, or details. In other words, never assume that your reader will understand what you have written just because you understand it. Don't be surprised if you have to go through several drafts before you are satisfied that what you have written is as you want it.

The correction chart that appears on the inside front cover will guide you in what to look for as you revise. Quite possibly a fresh look at your paper may reveal a flaw in your outline, as well as in your first draft. If so, don't hesitate to make changes in the outline. Like the first draft, the outline is only a means to an end—the end being a finished piece of writing that you are satisfied with.

The annotated theme that follows, on the Robin Hood legend, is the one that has been taking shape throughout this chapter. It illustrates the principles of unity and coherence you have been working with from the beginning. Comments in the left margin point out the main structural pieces in the total framework of the theme and suggest how these work together. Comments in the right margin identify major and minor supporting materials and indicate whether they are detail, illustration, or reason. The roman numerals relate the paragraphs of the body to the major topics of the outline.

The Robin Hood theme is about 750 words long: the introduction approximately 50 words, the body 650, the conclusion 50. The introduction precedes the body and contains the thesis (controlling) idea for the theme as a whole. The first sentence of the body introduces the major section of the paper, contains the controlling idea for that body, and relates the material of the body to the thesis sentence in the introduction. Each paragraph in the body has its own topic sentence and controlling idea that relates not only to the topic sentence of the body but also to the thesis sentence for closer unity. The various thought units and grammatical parts of the paragraph function much as each of the parts of a telescope slide within each other when it is closed.

Paragraphs III and IV form a unit dealing with two forests. The first sentence of paragraph III serves as topic sentence with its controlling idea *(shared)* of the unit. Paragraph III also has its own topic sentence and controlling idea, as does paragraph IV. Thus the unit through its own controlling idea is closely linked to the topic sentence of the body, and each of its two parts through their controlling ideas is in unity with the topic sentence of the unit as a whole. The controlling ideas of paragraphs V and VI are compound and basically the same, paragraph V applying them to Robin Hood, paragraph VI to Little John. Moreover, the two paragraphs taken together are essentially two parts of a comparison. The five paragraphs of the body are arranged in geographical (space) order from Nottingham north and west to Wakefield and then southwest to Hathersage and southeast to Nottingham.

The conclusion ends the discussion simply by offering the reader two choices already suggested in the introduction.

Following the Robin Hood theme is one on the topic of pollution. It is somewhat shorter and less complex in development. It may be used in addition to, or in place of, the Robin Hood theme as an example. And finally, the theme on Shakespeare's income is provided without the authors' analysis.

Analysis by Sentences	BACK TO ROBIN HOOD AND LITTLE JOHN	Type of Sentence
INTRODUCTION I. 1 Thesis sentence with *thesis idea*: identification with Robin Hood and Little John possible on certain conditions. 2 Statement of conditions.	I. [1]Identifying with Robin Hood and his lieutenant Little John is entirely possible for anyone willing to suppose them real. [2]It requires imaginative acceptance of materials, though largely traditional and fictitious, long approved by scholars of medieval legendists.	1 Thesis sentence/reason 2 Important qualification of thesis sentence; thus major support/reason
BODY II. 1 Topic sentence of the body of the theme (¶s II–IV) with its controlling idea (CI): *prevalent*. Directly supports the thesis idea in ¶ I.1–2. 2 Topic sentence of ¶ II (first of body of theme) with CI *lore*. Supports CI *prevalent* in ¶ II.1. 3–7 Support CI *lore* in this paragraph and *prevalent* in ¶ II.1.	II. [1]Evidence of Robin Hood is prevalent in North Central England, particularly in Nottinghamshire, Yorkshire, and Derbyshire. [2]Nottingham at the southern tip of the shire is especially rich in Robin Hood lore. [3]In caves beneath its streets Robin and his companions often sought refuge from the Sheriff. [4]One day Little John saved Will Stutely from the Constable, who was carting him off for hanging. [5]At one October fair the Sheriff of Nottingham proclaimed an archery contest to lure Robin into the city, but he failed to appear. [6]Instead, Little John competed against 800 foresters and won the golden arrow with shaft of silver white. [7]In the city's Council Tower the clock with the booming voice is affectionately called "Little John."	1 Major support for thesis sentence/detail 2 Major support for topic sentence of body/detail 3 Major support for topic sentence of ¶ II/ detail 4. Major support for topic sentence of ¶ II/detail 5–6 Major support for topic sentence of ¶ II/illustration 7 Major support of topic sentence of ¶ II/detail
III. 1 Topic sentence for a unit of two paragraphs (III–IV). CI of unit is *shared*. It controls material admitted to both paragraphs, and directly supports CI in ¶ II.1. 2 Topic sentence of ¶ III. Compound CI: *refuge* and *challenge*. Paragraph deals with Barnsdale alone. Supports CI in ¶ II.1. 3 Supports CI (extent of *refuge*). 4–7 Support CI *challenge*.	III. [1]Most adventures of Robin Hood and Little John were shared by Sherwood Forest, a few miles north of Nottingham, and by Barnsdale Forest, thirty miles beyond Sherwood. [2]During the Middle Ages Barnsdale, though small, was the first refuge of Robin Hood and therefore a challenge to all who entered it. [3]It extended from Skellbrook six miles north to the Went River, from Askern five miles west to Badsworth. [4]Thirteenth-century bishops and merchants carrying valuables often traveled under guard of eight to twenty archers. [5]One day Robin met and taunted a stranger to a contest with bow and arrow. [6]His long yew bow and gray goose-feathered shaft were a match for Robin, who had to split the stranger's arrow in the target to win. [7]The man called himself John Little, but the men of Barnsdale nicknamed him Little John.	1 major support for topic sentence of body/detail 2 Major support for CI in ¶ III.1/detail 3 Major support for topic sentence of ¶ III/detail 4 Major support for topic sentence of ¶ III/detail 5–7 Major support for topic sentence of ¶ III/illustration
IV. 1 Topic sentence of ¶ IV with CI: *activities*. Directly supports CI in ¶ III.1 and in II.1. Paragraph deals with Sherwood alone.	IV. [1]In time, Sherwood Forest, six times larger than Barnsdale, became best known for activities of the Robin Hood band. [2]Stretching from Nottingham north to Worksop, and from Chesterfield east to Newark, including 100,000	1 Major support for CI in ¶ III.1/detail 2 Major support for topic sentence of ¶ IV/detail

acres in Nottinghamshire alone, it provided ample area for robbing the rich and hiding quickly afterward. [3]At Edwinstowe, center of Sherwood, Robin married Maid Marion. [4]Three-quarters of a mile north of the village stood the 1400-year-old Major Oak, thirty feet in circumference, where Robin Hood and a dozen men hid from the Sheriff. [5]Once after a Greenwood dinner on the King's venison, Little John relieved the Constable of 300 pounds, and later Robin took 500 pounds from the 1,500 in gold and silver collected in fines and rentals by the Bishop of Hereford.

V [1]The deaths of Robin Hood and Little John are patterned with intrigue and loyal friendship. [2]In December 1247, when Robin became ill, Little John took him to Kirklees Priory, two miles east of Brighouse, Yorkshire, to be bled by his cousin the Prioress. [3]In collusion with her lover, she severed an artery in his arm. [4]Realizing he was dying, Robin blew three blasts on his horn, and Little John, awaiting his master in the Greenwood, rushed to his aid. [5]Though Robin Hood shot an arrow to locate his grave site, the Prioress buried him 650 yards beyond the Gatehouse (near the present highway). [6]Little John placed the gravestone—some 750 years ago.

VI [1]Forty miles south at Hathersage, Derbyshire, loyalties and intrigue likewise were prompted by the death of Little John. [2]Someone buried him in the yard of a twelfth-century church. [3]Today his ten-foot grave is covered with white daisies and enclosed by a low, spiked iron fence. [4]Its marker reads, "Here lies buried Little John, the friend & lieutenant of Robin Hood. [5]He died in a cottage to the east of the churchyard." [6]His six-foot bow, arrows, and cuirass, once in the church, have disappeared. [7]In 1784 the master of Cannon Hall nearby opened the grave and found a thigh bone 29 inches long. [8]Later it was buried under a tree, but no one knows which one.

VII [1]Those who follow the medieval routes of the Robin Hood legend to Hathersage face two alternatives. [2]Some see Robin and his men only as figures in tales of minstrel imagination. [3]Others hear three blasts on a distant horn and a deep-voiced bell echo against the hillside.

---

2 Supports CI: *activities* in this ¶; continues extent of "refuge" in ¶ III.2–3.
3–5 Support CI: *activities*.

V. 1 Topic sentence for a unit of two paragraphs (V–VI). Compound CI of unit: basic ideas of "loyalty" and "intrigue." This ¶ tells of Robin.
2 Supports CI: *loyal friendship*.
3 Supports CI: *intrigue*.
4 Supports CI: *loyal friendship*.
5 Supports CI: *intrigue*.
6 Supports CI: *loyal friendship*.

VI. 1 Topic sentence of ¶ VI with compound CI: *loyalties* and *intrigue*. (The controlling ideas of ¶ VI are basically those of ¶ V but are reversed for variety.)
2–5 Support CI: *loyalties*.
6–7 Support CI: *intrigue*.
8 Supports (probably) CI: *loyalties*.

CONCLUSION
VII. 1 Topic sentence of ¶ VII with CI: *alternatives*. Supports ¶ I.1–2.
2 Supports CI: *alternatives*.
3 Supports CI: *alternatives*.

---

3 Major support for topic sentence of ¶ IV/detail
4 Major support for topic sentence of ¶ IV/detail
5 Major support for topic sentence of ¶ IV/illustration

1 Major support for topic sentence of body/reason
2–6 Major support for topic sentence of ¶ V/illustration (2, part of 4, 6 stress "loyal friendship"), 3, part of 4, 5 stress "intrigue." But the illustration *as a whole* supports CI: *intrigue* leading to Robin Hood's death.)

1 Major support for topic sentence of body/reason
2 Major support for topic sentence and CI: *loyalties* of ¶ VI/detail
3 Major support for topic sentence and CI: *loyalties* of ¶ VI/detail
4–5 Major support for topic sentence and CI: *loyalties* of ¶ VI/detail
6 Major support for topic sentence and CI: *intrigue* of ¶ VI/detail
7 Major support for topic sentence and CI: *intrigue* of ¶ VI/detail

1 Major support of thesis sentence/reason
2 Major support for topic sentence of ¶ VII/detail
3 Major support for topic sentence of ¶ VII/detail

Analysis by Sentences

I. 1 Thesis sentence of the body of the theme (¶'s I–III) with CI (*destroy* man's environment and man).

2 Topic sentence of ¶ I with CI (*fouls water*) supports *environment* and *man*. "First" is transitional.

3–4 Directly support CI in sentence 2 (*fouls water*) and indirectly CI in ¶ I, sentence 1.

5–8 Support sentences 3–4 (toxic waste); also CI (fouls water) in ¶ I, sentence 2.

II. 1 Topic sentence of ¶ with CI *air* (as agent of destruction). Supports CI: *environment* and *man* in ¶ I, sentence 1. "Second" is transitional.

2–9 Directly support CI: *air* (as agent of destruction) in sentence 1 and indirectly support CI in ¶ I, sentence 1.

III. 1 Topic sentence of ¶ III with CI *land* (the analogy being based on the disarray and contamination of both). Supports thesis idea in ¶ I, sentence 1.

2–3 Continue the analogy

4 Continues image of ¶ I, sentence 1 and ¶ II, sentence 1. Theme ends with implication of man's own responsibility.

PUBLIC ENEMY NO. 2

I. ¹Many people insist that pollution is destroying not only man's environment but man himself. ²First, it fouls the water upon which all life depends. ³Raw sewage is pumped into nearby bodies of water as convenient and inexpensive areas of disposal. ⁴It will eventually destroy both their physical existence and their aesthetic beauty. ⁵Major rivers wash mercury poisons, insecticides, and even radioactive substances drained from their watersheds into nearby lakes and oceans. ⁶The Hudson River in many places is now an eyesore. ⁷The Mississippi is choked with refuse and noxious debris. ⁸The shores of Lake Erie are strewn with bloated fish that have died from poisons and a lack of oxygen.

II. ¹Second, the air as well as water has become a potential agent of destruction. ²Millions of machines, automobiles, airplanes, trucks, buses, and motorcycles spew out tons of carbon monoxide. ³The deadly gas fills the atmosphere and settles in garages and tunnels. ⁴The upper air carries toxic smoke belched from industrial smokestacks. ⁵Radioactive particles explode into the air from nuclear test sites in many parts of the world. ⁶Pesticides sprayed by man or from cropdusting planes fall on insects, food, animals, and man. ⁷Toxic materials increasingly endanger birds and animals through poisoned foods and water. ⁸Indirectly, the same poisons attack man worldwide. ⁹Foglike, these poisons infiltrate and destroy birds, animals, and man himself, for walls and wishes do not keep them away.

III. ¹Finally, many land areas in the United States have come to resemble the floor of an old attic. ²Like bundles of yellowed magazines from generations of hoarders, junked automobiles, refrigerators, and stoves rust away in silence and neglect. ³Discarded products made of iron, steel, aluminum, tin, and plastic lie strewn in neglected litter, defacing the land. ⁴Even the soil itself, infiltrated by residues from noxious debris and chemical contaminants, is carried by air and rain to rest at last at man's own feet.

Type of Sentence

I. 1 Thesis sentence/reason

2 Major support for topic sentence/reason

3 Minor support for sentence 2/illustration

4 Minor support for sentence 3/illustration

5 Major support for sentence 2/illustration

6–8 Minor support for sentence 2/reason

II. 1 Topic sentence/reason

2 Major support for topic sentence/illustration

3–6 Major support for sentence 2/illustration

7–8 Major support for sentence 2/reason

9 Major support for sentence 8/illustration

III. 1 Topic sentence/reason

2–3 Major support for topic sentence/detail

4 Major support for topic sentence/illustration

Analysis by Sentences

WHAT WAS SHAKESPEARE'S INCOME?

Oh to be in England now that April's there

INTRODUCTION

I. ¹Browning, Chaucer, and Shakespeare all had a thing for April. ²Browning praised it from a ship at sea, Chaucer started his Canterbury pilgrimage in April, and Shakespeare must have doted on it—he was born and buried in April. ³As for me, it's the month of income tax day! ⁴When I was licking the stamp recently to mail in my tax, my curiosity piqued me. ⁵I got to wondering just how much Shakespeare paid his "Uncle Sam" on April 15th. ⁶I produced a pencil and note paper, and began picking my memory to determine, if I could, how Bill Shakespeare fared on *his* April 15th. ⁷Plucking the pigeonholes of my memory proved he fared as well as I. ⁸The Parish Register in Trinity Church, Stratford-on-Avon, records for April 26, 1564 the baptism of "Gulielmus filius Johannes Shakespere"—William son of John Shakespere. ⁹Fifty-two years later to the day, he returned to the same church for an honorable burial beneath a stone in the chancel. ¹⁰Between those dates he gave the world 37 plays and a fair amount of poetry. ¹¹The world has venerated him ever since. ¹²Ben Jonson, fellow poet and dramatist, summed it up in one line: "He was not of an age, but for all time!"

BODY

II. ¹Any computation of a man's financial state in the reigns of Queen Elizabeth and King James I must accept data necessarily beggared by insufficient facts. ²Let's consider Shakespeare's activities, then, between January 1, 1603 and late fall of 1611, when he retired. ³Some evidence is available: he wrote and sold plays, he was an actor and share holder (owner) in the Globe and Blackfriars theaters; he and others entertained at Court. ⁴He also had business interests in Stratford and in Warwickshire.

WHAT WAS SHAKESPEARE'S INCOME?

III. [1]Although the Globe burned down in 1613, its size, stages, galleries, and admission fees can be gauged from those of the Fortune Theater modeled on it. [2]It will be simplest to estimate Shakespeare's income on the basis of a full house for each of 200 performances a year, keeping in mind that from his earnings as part owner (sharer) in two theaters he would have shared in all operating expenses.

IV. [1]Location, weather, and lighting often determined the actual performance of a play, as much as city officials. [2]The Globe was located on the Bankside in the Liberty of the Clink, Southwark, some distance upstream from London Bridge. (A brewery is there now.) [3]Plays were given only in the afternoon in fair weather, for the Globe was without artificial lighting and a roof. [4]Even then, city officials closed all theaters during plague, Lent, and Sunday. [5]A flag flew from the Globe's tower whenever a play was on. [6]Patrons crossed the River Thames by boat continuing by foot across marshy land. [7]Shakespeare has hinted the performance of a play at the Globe took "two hours' traffic of the stage."

V. [1]A capacity audience at the Globe depended on variables. [2]One scholar estimated attendance on his knowledge of anatomy and the hand-held calculator: a full house numbered 2,345: 818 standing in the pit, the ground area on three sides of a protruding, apron-like stage; 509 seated in each of three galleries. [3]Admission was based on where a patron sat or stood: in the pit, groundlings paid one pence or penny; patrons in the lowest gallery, three pennies; in each of the two upper galleries, two pennies. [4]A full house brought in 4,381 pennies or $700 (the penny being worth about 16 cents).

VI. [1]On command, company personnel performed at the Court of James I in Westminster, as they had for Queen Elizabeth, at an estimated annual income of $5,240. [2]The Globe actors soon became the King's Men. [3]Royal patronage exempted them from certain humiliating charges often brought by the City Fathers against itinerant peddlers, jugglers, and actors, and assured them of popularity and additional income.

VII. [1]In the summer of 1608 they also acquired Blackfriars Theater, a major advantage for the King's Men. [2]It was situated in the southwest corner of the walled City of London. [3]They leased it for $1,600 a year and spent about $36,000 renovating it. [4]When completed, Blackfriars seated some 600 people, was roofed, and had artificial lighting. [5]Now able to perform at night and during the winter, the company attracted a better clientele at higher prices. [6]Receipts from a capacity audience at Blackfriars were two-and-a-half times those from the Globe, or $1,750. [7]Beginning in 1609 the company gave about 100 performances in each theater annually.

VIII. [1]Financially, the King's Men were now much better off. [2]They were organized into two groups: sharers (or owners) and actors. [3]From 1603 to 1612 their income from the Globe—$700 (one day's box office) times 200 (performances a year) times 9 (years) was $1,050,000. [4]From the Court, they received $5,240 (annual increment) times 9 (years) was $47,160. [5]Their total income then was $1,097,160. [6]As a sharer, Shakespeare received one-tenth of half of the total take ($54,858) and as an actor one-seventh of the other half ($78,368) for a nine-year income of $133,226 from the Globe and the Court. [7]From 1609 to 1612, when he retired, gate receipts from Blackfriars were $525,000. [8]By now Shakespeare probably received one-seventh of each half, or $75,000. [9]Shake-

Analysis by Sentences

Type of Sentence

WHAT WAS SHAKESPEARE'S INCOME?

speare was also a prominent playwright. [10]Between 1603 and 1612 he wrote ten plays for the King's Men, probably at $320 or more apiece. [11]Imagine $320 for a *Hamlet* or a *Lear!* [12]Each sale of a play added to his other income.

IX. [1]We can now estimate that Shakespeare's total income from the Globe, Blackfriars, and Court as sharer, actor, and playwright from 1603 to 1612 was $211,426. [2]His average annual income was approximately $23,500. [3]So, come April, Gulielmus filius Johannes Shakespere or William Shakespeare, *Gent.* (allowed by his father's coat of arms) faced His Majesty's Form 1040. [4]He could claim two exemptions (he and Anne were under sixty-five) and the standard deduction of 15% or $2,000 (Shakespeare seems not overly generous to the church or Stratford's United Way campaign). [5]His taxable income came to a comfortable $23,500—plus. [6]The tax itself was a greedy $3,149, or maybe—more?!

CONCLUSION

X. [1]We must remember that these figures are based on estimated total income from Shakespeare's association with the theaters and the Court without regard to expenses that he must have shared. [2]Moreover, no income from his investments in Stratford and Warwickshire are included. [3]If, perchance, you were to walk quietly behind St. Paul's cathedral just before midnight on April 15th, very possibly you would see Shakespeare emerge from the Mermaid Tavern, a bit tipsy, perhaps, and at the last moment drop his tax return with a check enclosed into a carrier's mailpouch nearby. [4]Listening ever so attentively, you might even hear familiar words: "Oh, my ducats! My ducats!" [5]A moment's hesitation, then— "Who steals my purse, steals trash." [6]Then, finally, very despondently:

"Oh Shylock, how well knew ye:
Poor, poor Iago, how ill did thee!"(67)

Topics for Paragraphs and Short Papers

Each of the following topics *may* be suitable for a short paper or, with limitation, a paragraph. It is therefore important that you analyze each topic that you undertake to write about with the concept of limitation in mind.

1. Fighting Pollution
2. Equal Pay for Equal Work
3. Drag Racing
4. Library Noises
5. City Streets after a Hard Winter
6. Aftermath of a Flood
7. Thoughts while Jogging
8. The Generation Gap
9. Ten-Speed Bike Maintenance
10. Management by Crisis
11. How Not to Buy a Used Car
12. The Shopping Center on Saturday Afternoon
13. What Is Insulting about Television Commercials
14. The Oil Glut
15. Clutter in the Cellar
16. An Egoist
17. Silicon Valley

18. New Friends and Old
19. The Future in Outer Space
20. A Change in Study Habits
21. Advantages and Disadvantages of a Small College
22. Waiting at an Air Terminal
23. Air Travel Versus Bus Travel
24. Driving a Car in Europe
25. The Importance of Being Oneself
26. The Most Influential Person of the Twentieth Century
27. Picking a Winner with Statistics
28. Using Jumper Cables
29. Word Processing and the Typewriter
30. Secrets in the Attic
31. Comforts of Air Conditioning in a Car
32. Advantages and Disadvantages of Buying a Car Abroad
33. Learning to Program
34. Playing Games on the Computer
35. Water Never Runs Uphill
36. An Important Lesson
37. Penny Wise, Pound Foolish
38. The Early Bird Gets the Worm
39. Many Hands Make Light Work
40. Misery Loves Company
41. A Bird in the Hand is Worth Two in the Bush
42. The Hill Is Greener on the Other Side
43. Still Water Runs Deep
44. Ignorance Is Bliss
45. VCR Films
46. Fast-Food Chain Logos
47. Rights and Responsibilities
48. Great Britain Resembles a Sitting Dog

49. Electrical Appliances Have Replaced Servants
50. The Appeal of the Covers of Travel Magazines
51. Surf's Up!
52. Unreturned Phone Calls
53. Three Jumps Ahead of the Bill Collector
54. Bull and Bear Markets
55. The Rites of Spring
56. Raking Leaves on a Windy Day
57. Challenges of Political Office
58. On Finding Homes for a Litter of Puppies
59. The Dog or Cat as a Preferable Pet
60. Used Book Stores
61. Dealing with a Cantankerous Boss
62. The Importance of Rules
63. The New Craze
64. Crabgrass Control
65. Car Names to Catch the Public Fancy
66. Air Bags in Cars or Not
67. The Longest Minute I Ever Lived
68. Attitudes toward Nuclear Power
69. Life in a Distant Computer
70. The Joy of Junk Food
71. Selecting Dinner from an Expensive Menu
72. Friendship Is Like a Feather Bed
73. Ban the Bomb!
74. "Doing" One's Income Taxes
75. The Latest in Students' Hair Fashions
76. Mom 'n' Pop Stores
77. Contrasting Customers on a Paper Route
78. Similarities between Music and Language
79. Home Is Where the Heart Is

80.   What Makes a Public Event Newsworthy?

81.   Point of Purchase (POP) Merchandising

82.   Tedious Public Figures

83.   Analogy to the Human Skeleton

84.   Fences Make Good Neighbors

85.   Teaching Is an Ego Trip

86.   How to Market Raisins

87.   The Fascination of Maps

88.   Amorality

89.   The Last Thirty Seconds of the Championship Game

90.   Plagiarism

91.   Back to Basics!

92.   What Is an Antique?

93.   Comparison (Or Contrast) of the Speaking Styles of Two American Presidents

94.   Similarities between Two Breeds of Dogs

95.   Public Outrage

96.   How to Mend Something That Has Been Broken

97.   The Ideal Home

98.   Justice Is Often Blind

99.   His Complaints Are Like a Broken Record

100.   Civil Disobedience—A Definition

Concise Guide to Punctuation

This concise guide to punctuation will help you avoid some common errors as you write your paragraphs or as you revise them. Only the most common punctuation problems are treated here. For other uses of punctuation marks, consult a handbook.

The Comma

Use a comma to separate an introductory word, phrase, or clause from the rest of the sentence:

- *Well,* we may as well get started. [mild interjection]
- *After a long series of delays,* the plane was cleared for takeoff. [prepositional phrase]
- *Hoping to catch the enemy off guard,* the general ordered a surprise attack. [participial phrase]
- *After hearing the distant sound of battle,* the general ordered an attack. [prepositional phrase with gerund]
- *Although the weather was bad,* the parade started right on schedule. [introductory dependent clause]

NOTE: No comma is needed after a short introductory prepositional phrase, except to avoid misreading a sentence:

- *After eating,* the duck waddled off.
- *On Fridays* I have no morning classes.

Use a comma between independent clauses joined by a coordinate conjunction:

- The critics ridiculed the novel, but it soon became a popular success.

Use a comma between items in a series:

- Griffins, unicorns, and centaurs are mythical beasts.
- The book can be obtained in bookstores, at newsstands, and by mail order.

NOTE: Do not use a comma when the connecting word *and* or *or* is repeated between each pair of items:

- You can reach the resort by car or plane or boat.

Use commas to set off nonessential elements:

- The book, which was originally written in Rumanian, was soon available in several languages. [nonessential clause]
- There must, he thought to himself, be an easier way. [parenthetical expression]
- Mr. Packard, the headmaster, presented the award. [appositive]

NOTE: Do not set off elements that are essential to the meaning of the sentence:

- None of us can read a book *that is written in Rumanian.*
- My uncle *Al* is the youngest of five brothers.
- The man *about whom I am talking* is in the house.

Use a comma or commas to separate a direct quotation from such explanatory words as *he said* or *she asked* unless a question mark or exclamation point is used:

- "I'm just one hundred and one, five months, and a day," the Queen remarked.
- "Where is Jones?" asked the coach. [*But* The coach asked, "Where is Jones?"]

- "I can't believe that!" said Alice.
- "This cat," declared the policeman, "belongs to Mr. Jones."
- Martin Luther King intoned, "I have a dream."

The Semicolon

Use a semicolon between independent clauses not joined by the coordinate conjunctions *(and, or, but, nor).*

- Grammar is the study of the system of a language; usage is concerned with choices within that system.
- The mayor continued to insist that she had not yet decided about running for reelection; however, her public statements began to sound more and more like campaign speeches.

Use a semicolon between items in a series when the items contain commas:

- The quartet consists of George Kemp and Alicia Perez, violinists; Alba Hyk, viola; and Gerald Sommers, cello.

The Colon

Use a colon to introduce a series of items, especially after a clause that is grammatically complete:

- The room was a mixture of colors: red, orange, blue, pink.

Use a colon after *the following, as follows,* and similar words, and before a long quotation or explanation:

- Word the list as follows: women first, men next, boys and girls last.
- The colonel had but one idea in mind: to storm the fort, capture its commander, send word back to his superior, and occupy the site until reinforcements arrived.

NOTE: Avoid using a colon immediately after any form of the verbs *be, seem, appear:*

- The girls who assisted me were Fran and Mary.

Quotation Marks

Use quotation marks to enclose the exact words of a speaker or writer. Note the following conventional practices:

1. An interrupted quotation has quotation marks around only the quoted words.
   "There's no use trying," Alice said. "One can't believe impossible things."

2. A quotation of several sentences takes quotation marks only at the beginning of the first sentence and at the end of the last.
   Caesar said, "I came. I saw. I conquered."

3. A quotation of several paragraphs takes quotation marks at the beginning of each paragraph but at the end of only the last paragraph.

4. Omission of words within a quotation is shown by means of a set of three periods (called an *ellipsis*): "The human species . . . is composed of two distinct races, the men who borrow and the men who lend." (Charles Lamb)

5. Insertion of a word within a quotation (by someone other than the author of the quoted matter) is shown by brackets:
   "Whatever question there may be of his [Thoreau's] talent, there can be none, I think, of his genius." (Henry James)

6. Quoted lines of poetry are usually not enclosed in quotation marks, especially when there are several lines. They are indented as a unit under the text of the writer who is quoting them.

7. Quotations within quotations are indicated by single quotation marks within the regular double ones:
   She asked, "Who said, 'Practice makes perfect'?" [Note the position of each mark of punctuation in this sentence.]

Use quotation marks in combination with other marks in these ways:

1. Place periods and commas inside the quotation marks:
   "Yes," he said. "I'll do what I can."

2. Place colons and semicolons outside the quotation marks:
   The argument concerned the meaning of "cruel and unusual punishment"; it did not include any specific type of punishment.

3. Place question marks, exclamation points, and dashes inside the quotation marks when they clearly belong with the quoted material; place

them outside when they refer to the rest of the sentence. Compare the following:

She asked, "When do we start?"	Did he sing "Old Man River"?
"Stop!" the guard shouted.	How surprised we were to hear her say, "I don't know"!

Quotation Marks and Underlining (Equivalent to "Italics" in Handwritten Composition)

Use underlining for

1. Titles of books, plays, long poems, and major works of art generally: *Roots, Hamlet, Iliad, La Gioconda.*
2. Names of ships, planes, trains, and so on: *Titanic, Spirit of St. Louis, The Chief.*
3. Foreign words not yet thoroughly anglicized: *modus vivendi, bon appétit.*
4. Words, letters, and symbols referred to as such: Do you pronounce *aunt* and *ant* the same?
   Cross your *t*'s and dot your *i*'s.
   Is this a *1* or a *7?*

Use quotation marks for

1. Titles of short stories, songs, short poems, and short works generally: "The Black Cat," "The Star Spangled Banner," "Old Ironsides," Lincoln's "Gettysburg Address."
2. The definition of a word:
   Gutsy means "courageous."

Parentheses

Use parentheses to enclose incidental material:

- During the first several years of the mortgage, the principal is reduced only slightly (see Chart C).

Brackets

Use brackets to enclose editorial remarks or words that you insert in a direct quotation:

- "From a distance it [fear] is something; nearby it is nothing." (La Fontaine)

The Dash

Use a dash to show a sudden break in thought:

- He could—and undoubtedly should—have waited for reinforcements.

Use a dash to set off parenthetical elements when you want to give the interpolated material special emphasis:

- The murder—the possibility of suicide had been ruled out—was the only topic of conversation in the village.

Question Mark

Use a question mark after a direct question:

- Are you going to the game?
- Did she ask, "Who made the pies?"
- Did you hear him say, "I am going"?
- Kevin was born in 1980(?).
- "Who shot the bear?" she asked.

Acknowledgments

Grateful acknowledgment is made for use of the following material, listed in order of appearance in the text.

1. Margaret Truman, *Women of Courage,* William Morrow & Co, Inc., 1976, p. 30.
2. Rutherford Platt, *The River of Life,* Simon & Schuster, Inc., 1956, p. 284. Originally printed by The Grolier Society, *The Book of Knowledge Annual,* © 1955.
3. Richard Le Gallienne, *The Romantic 90's,* Doubleday, 1925, p. 55.
4. Barbara W. Tuchman, *The Guns of August,* Macmillan, Inc., 1962, p. 1.
5. Leo A. Borah, "Montana," *National Geographic Magazine,* June 1950, p. 693. © 1950.
6. George Santayana, *The Sense of Beauty,* Charles Scribner's Sons, 1896, p. 169.
7. J. Bronowski, "The Creative Process," *Scientific American,* September 1958, pp. 60, 62.
8. Ernest Earnest, "Must the TV Technicians Take Over the Colleges?," *AAUP Bulletin,* Autumn 1958, p. 583.
9. Harry Golden, *Only in America,* World Publishing Company, 1958, p. 240. © 1958, 1957, 1956, 1955, 1954, 1953, 1951, 1949, 1948, 1944 by Harry Golden. Published by arrangement with the World Publishing Company (now Harcourt Brace Jovanovich).
10. Copyright 1959 by Consumers Union of U.S., Inc., Mount Vernon, NY 10553. Excerpted by permission from *Consumer Reports,* November, 1959.

11. Deems Taylor, *Of Men and Music,* Simon & Schuster, 1937, p. 6.

12. *New York Times,* 13 April 1958, section 4, p. 1.

13. Vance Packard, "The Pursuit of Status," *Look,* 28 April 1959, p. 92.

14. Eric Hoffer, "The Role of the Undesirables," *Harper's Magazine,* December 1952, pp. 80–81.

15. Rachel Carson, *The Silent Spring,* Houghton Mifflin Company, 1962, p. 93.

16. Lloyd Morris, *Incredible New York,* Random House, Inc., 1951.

17. Penelope McMillan, "Women and Tranquilizers," *Ladies' Home Journal,* November 1976, p. 166. © 1976, Downe Publishing, Inc. Reprinted with permission of *Ladies' Home Journal.*

18. Donna Stansby, a student.

19. Selma H. Fraiberg, *The Magic Years,* Charles Scribner's Sons, 1959, p. 121.

20. Mary Ellen Chase, "Why Teach Literature?" *Literature Today* (no. 5), Houghton Mifflin Company, 1966, p. 5.

21. From *Farewell to Sport,* by Paul Gallico. Copyright 1938 and renewed 1966 by Paul Gallico. Reprinted by permission of Alfred A. Knopf, Inc.

22. C. Northcote Parkinson, *Parkinson's Law,* pamphlet reprinted from *The Economist,* 19 November 1955, p. 3.

23. Aaron Copland, *What to Listen for in Music,* McGraw-Hill Book Company, 1957, rev. ed., pp. 9–10.

24. Maynard Kniskern, editorial, Springfield (Ohio) *Sun,* 23 October 1962, p. 6.

25. "Home Remedy," *The New Yorker,* 10 June 1950, p. 21.

26. E. B. White, *Here Is New York,* Harper & Row, Publishers, 1949, pp. 24–25.

27. Carol A. Norton, "Black Women in Corporate America," *Ebony,* November 1975, p. 108. Reprinted by permission of *Ebony* Magazine, © 1975 by Johnson Publishing Company, Inc.

28. Phyllis McGinley, *The Province of the Heart,* The Viking Press, Inc., 1951.

29. Thomas N. Carmichael, "Waterloo: 1815," *Life,* 11 June 1965, p. 86. © Time Inc.

30. Jerome Ellison, "American Disgrace: Cheating," *The Saturday Evening*

Post, 9 January 1960, p. 58. Reprinted from *The Saturday Evening Post* © 1960, The Curtis Publishing Company.

31. *Changing Times,* November 1976, p. 20. Reprinted with permission from *Changing Times* Magazine, © 1976 Kiplinger Washington Editors, Inc., November, 1976.

32. Virginia Snitlow, "The Mushroom Cloud," *The Western Political Quarterly,* December 1958, p. 875. Reprinted by permission of the University of Utah, copyright owners.

33. Samuel Eliot Morison, "Prescott, the American Thucydides," *Atlantic Monthly,* November 1957, p. 170.

34. Rachel Carson, *The Sea Around Us,* Oxford University Press, 1961, rev. ed., p 107.

35. Joseph Conrad, "The Lagoon," *Complete Works of Joseph Conrad,* Doubleday, 1924, VIII, 189. By permission of Messrs. J. M. Dent & Sons, Ltd., and the Trustees of the Joseph Conrad Estate.

36. Alfred Hooper, *Makers of Mathematics,* Random House, Inc., 1948, p. 30. © by Random House, Inc.

37. Frederick E. Faverty, *Your Literary Heritage,* p. 24, © 1959 by Frederick E. Faverty. Published by J. B. Lippincott Company.

38. Elizabeth A. Moise, "Turnaround Time in West Virginia," *National Geographic,* June 1976, p. 755.

39. Mario Pei, "English in 2061: A Forecast," *Saturday Review,* 14 January 1961, p. 13.

40. Robert M. Hutchins, "What Is a General Education?" *Harper's Magazine,* November 1936.

41. Virginia Snitlow, "The Mushroom Cloud," *The Western Political Quarterly,* December 1958, p. 882. Reprinted by permission of the University of Utah, copyright owners.

42. Adapted from Sanche de Gramont, *The French: Portrait of a People,* G. P. Putnam's Sons. © 1969 by Sanche de Gramont.

43. Lee DuBridge, "Science—the Endless Adventure." Reprinted with permission from *Bulletin of the Atomic Scientists,* March 1957, p. 75. © 1965 by the Educational Foundation for Nuclear Science, Inc.

44. James B. Conant, "Athletics: The Poison Ivy in Our Schools," *Look,* 17

January 1961, p. 58. By permission of the editors of *Look,* © 1961, Cowles Magazines & Broadcasting, Inc.

45. Arthur Miller, "The Family in Modern Drama," *Atlantic Monthly,* April 1956, p. 38.

46. John Garraty, *The Nature of Biography,* Alfred A Knopf, Inc., 1957, p. 28.

47. Russell Lynes, "Is There a Gentleman in the House?" *Look,* 9 June 1959, pp. 19–20.

48. James W. Johnson, *Logic and Rhetoric,* The Macmillan Publishing Company, Inc., 1962.

49. J. Harold Wilson and Robert S. Newdick, *The Craft of Exposition,* D.C. Heath & Company, 1933, pp. 12–13.

50. LeRoi Jones, *Home: Social Essays by LeRoi Jones,* William Morrow & Co., Inc., 1966.

51. Alan Simpson, "The Marks of an Educated Man," *Context,* I (Spring 1961), p. 4.

52. Carole Masley, a student.

53. Clifton Fadiman, "Ernest Hemingway: An American Byron," *The Nation,* 18 January 1933, p. 64.

54. Diane Grossett, a student.

55. Arthur Koestler, "The Anatomy of Snobbery," *The Anchor Review,* no. 1, Doubleday Anchor Books, 1955, p. 13. By permission of A.D. Peters and Company.

56. Wade Thompson, "My Crusade Against Football," *The Nation,* 11 April 1959, p. 313.

57. Robert Warnock and George K. Anderson, *The Ancient Foundations: Book One of the World in Literature,* Scott, Foresman and Company, 1950, p. 319.

58. Samuel Eliot Morison, *The Young Man Washington,* Harvard University Press, 1932, pp. 8–9.

59. Mary Ellen Chase, "Why Teach Literature?" *Literature Today* 5, Houghton Mifflin Company, 1966, p. 1.

60. Donald Culross Peattie, "Chlorophyll: The Sun Trap," *Flowering Earth,* © 1939 Donald Culross Peattie. Originally published by G.P. Putnam's Sons, p. 32. Reprinted by permission of Curtis Brown Assoc., Ltd.

61. Margaret Schlauch, *A Gift of Tongues,* The Viking Press, Inc., 1924, p. 111.

62. Joseph Vendryes, *Language: A Linguistic Introduction to History,* Alfred A. Knopf, 1925.

63. Victor Hugo, *Les Miserables,* 1862.

64. John Keats, *The Insolent Chariots,* pp. 12–13. © John Keats. Published by J. B. Lippincott Company.

65. Robert Louis Stevenson, "The Old Pacific Capital," *Works of Robert Louis Stevenson,* Charles Scribner's Sons, 1907. © 1892, XV, p. 149.

66. John Unterecker, "Poetry for the Perfectly Practical Man," *Columbia University Forum,* Winter 1959. Reprinted by permission from *The Columbia Forum.* Copyright 1959 by the Trustees of Columbia University in the City of New York. All rights reserved.

67. John W. Ostrom, "Shakespeare Pays His Income Tax," *The Baltimore Sun Magazine,* 2 February 1980.

▌Index